THE GENERALIST'S ADVANTAGE

How to Harness the Raw Power
of Cross-Disciplinary Thinking

JOE CURCILLO

The Generalist's Advantage
How to Harness the Raw Power of Cross-Disciplinary Thinking
by Joe Curcillo

Copyright © 2024 by Joe Curcillo

All rights reserved. No part of this book may be used or reproduced in any manner whatsoever without written permission except in the case of brief quotations embodied in critical articles and reviews.

For information, contact:
Synergy Thinkers Press

Harrisburg, Pennsylvania
www.TheGeneralistsAdvantage.com

ISBN: 978-1-7324856-2-4 (paperback)

First Edition

Printed in the United States of America

*Dedicated to my
wife and daughters.*

*They have been by my side
for all my life's ups and downs
and hard left turns.*

Contents

PREPARE

1. Finding Our Path: Multidisciplinarity in Focus 3

SEE MORE

2. Widening the Lens: a Grandfather, a Puppet, and a Poet 21
3. The Integrated Mindset: Thinking in Multiple Lanes 35
4. The Map: Becoming a Generalist 47
5. Lane Hoppers: Innovators, Integrators, and Disruptors 67

BE MORE

6. Be a Fox: Versatile, Adaptable, and Agile 91
7. The Brain: Debunking Myths and Maximizing Potential 117
8. Jack of All Trades: A More Elastic Mind 125
9. Decision-Making: A Mosaic of Experiences 149
10. The Strategist: Seeing the Future 173

LEARN MORE

11. Learning Mindset: One Superpower at a Time 199
12. The Books You Read: Beyond Boundaries 209
13. Lifelong Learner: New Skills Every Day! 217
14. The Instant Expert and Overcoming Imposter Syndrome 241

DO MORE

15. Multidisciplinary Teams: Orchestrating Success in Diverse Teams 255
16. A Productive Mix: The Power of Collaborative Teams 269
17. Breaking Down Silos: Fostering Cross-Disciplinary Thinking 289
18. Champions of Integration: Multidisciplinary Leaders 301
19. Embracing All Lanes: Your Symphony of Discovery 317

Acknowledgments 325

About the Author 327

PREPARE

1

Finding Our Path: Multidisciplinarity in Focus

You realize when you know how to think, it empowers you far beyond those who know only what to think.
— Neil deGrasse Tyson

I want to talk to you about living wide and living a multidisciplinary life.

Some might think that having one profession is enough. But what if I told you that, through being multidisciplinary, you can open doors to a new and exciting way of life? That by combining skills and knowledge from different fields you can create a unique and powerful approach to problem-solving, innovation, and success?

Being multidisciplinary means having the ability to adapt and learn new skills quickly. In today's world, where change is constant, being adaptable is crucial to keeping up with our fast-paced environment. It also helps to broaden your perspective and understand different viewpoints, leading to better decision-making.

Being multidisciplinary also opens up new career opportunities and expands your knowledge and success in your current career. You can combine your skills and expertise in different fields to create a unique set of offerings that no one else can provide.

Learning and mastering multiple disciplines will greatly improve the way you think. It allows you to see the world from different perspectives and encourages you to think critically and creatively. Continued learning allows you to enhance your problem-solving skills and helps you approach challenges in more creative and effective ways. Exposure to different fields will spark fresh ideas and inspire you to pursue new opportunities and paths. Your life journey will take you in new and exciting directions with each field you master.

Each new lane that you enter will enhance the way you work and live. It will increase your value as an employee or entrepreneur because you will bring new diverse skills and knowledge to the table. You will be inspired to use techniques and concepts from different fields to improve your work in your current profession. For example, a programmer with a background in psychology can create more intuitive and user-friendly interfaces than could someone who only knows how to write code.

Being multidisciplinary will enrich your life in countless other ways. Learning about new subjects will expand your horizons and give you a broader understanding of the world. It can also provide you with new hobbies and interests, leading to personal growth and fulfillment.

What This Book Is About

Throughout this book I will speak of generalists, multidisciplinaries, multidisciplinarians, and people who live in multiple lanes. To me, these terms are interchangeable. In essence, we are discussing those who see more, learn more, do more, and become more; people who have a broad understanding of a range of disciplines and can act based on that knowledge. These are the ones who are jacks-of-all-trades AND masters of integration, the cross disciplinary thinkers. Those who pull from their diverse knowledge to create innovative solutions to problems that require multiple perspectives. They are creative problem-solvers who see beyond the silos of specialization and can connect seemingly unrelated ideas and concepts.

Whether you know it or not, this is, or *could* be, you. This book is designed to inspire you to expand your grasp of unfamiliar topics and develop a deeper understanding of how they relate to your life.

By learning how to integrate new disciplines into your daily routine and live in multiple lanes, you will enhance your personal growth and create a more meaningful existence. Whether you want to improve your career prospects, build better relationships, or simply broaden your horizons, this book will guide you on your journey to self-improvement.

We'll explore the advantages of being a generalist, including the ability to think critically, communicate effectively, and adapt to change, and you'll gain a greater understanding of how cognitive thinking works, and how the skills and knowledge of a generalist can create better thought-out solutions.

You will also discover a powerful multidisciplinary approach to learning and thinking as well as the ability to develop a broad range of skills and knowledge, building networks across disciplines, and cultivating a willingness to take risks and experiment.

This book is for anyone who wants to become a more effective problem-solver, innovator, and forward-thinking strategist, regardless of your current area of specialization. It's for those who want to develop a broad range of skills and knowledge, and who are willing to embrace the challenges that come with being a generalist.

As we explore the benefits of being multidisciplinary, keep in mind that my goal is to inspire you to *live* in multiple lanes. Somewhere along the way, when you allow your disciplines to converge, you will discover the joy of cross-disciplinary thinking. Once you have done that you can harness its true power and do more than you ever dreamed was possible.

Let's take a look at the convergence of disciplines and what certain terms mean. There are the three thinking styles at play: multidisciplinary, interdisciplinary, and cross disciplinary.

Using a metaphor,[1] consider an architect who garners insight from diverse fields without melding them together—like employing acoustics, consulting with landscape designers, and using engineers for structure. This is *multidisciplinary*

---

[1] Metaphor inspired by Moti Nissani, Fruits, Salads, and Smoothies: A Working Definition of Interdisciplinarity, *The Journal of Educational Thought* (JET) / Revue de la Pensée Éducative, Vol. 29, No. 2 (August, 1995), pp. 121-128 (8 pages), Werklund School of Education, University of Calgary

thinking. It's akin to a fruit salad wherein all the different fruits are distinct in their properties, but they all work in harmony.

In contrast, consider an architect who designs a sustainable building, weaving environmental concepts into architectural ones, and blending the whole into the landscape. This is *interdisciplinary thinking*, the blending of diverse knowledge as seamlessly as a fruit smoothie. All the knowledge is shared and merged to create an entirely new result.

Think Frank Lloyd Wright. Fallingwater is a masterpiece. He had to take a multidisciplinary approach with engineers to achieve the daring structural feats evident in that iconic structure.

Then there was the interdisciplinary thinking that that integrates architecture with nature, art, engineering, and design, producing a unique synthesis.

Then he had the artistic challenge. For that he reached into another of his life's lanes, borrowing principles from art, specifically from Japanese aesthetics, and applied them to his architectural design. He found a solution that didn't require a deep dive into the Japanese art lane. He pulled in just enough conceptual knowledge to achieve a unique synergistic result, taking an idea that lived in one domain and introducing it into a new domain where the concept had never lived before, like Japanese aesthetics in the backwoods of Pennsylvania. Shear genius. Pure innovation.

Cross-disciplinary thinking is where the really cool and amazing stuff happens. Back to our metaphor: It's not a fruit smoothie. It's not a fruit salad. It's something brand new and innovative. It's so amazing that it brings to mind the idiom *the greatest thing since sliced bread*. (In my fruit metaphor, maybe it was the birth of the margarita?)

Harnessing the power of cross-disciplinary thinking will improve the way you think, work, and live. Once you have found yourself living in multiple lanes and working in multiple disciplines, reaching into another lane for an idea becomes second nature.

That is where this book wants you to go. That is the Generalist's Advantage!

I encourage you to explore new subjects and continue learning throughout your life. It's a thrilling experience, providing a sense of personal growth and discovery. However, for some of you, the idea of exploring uncharted territory can be intimidating or overwhelming. But keep your hands and feet inside the vehicle. I assure you this multidisciplinary ride will end in a safe, happy, and incredibly exciting place. You will find a new you.

What This Book Is NOT About

This book is not a condemnation of specialization. It unequivocally does not intend to criticize or diminish the importance of specialists. It's evident that we rely on experts with honed skills in various fields for our well-being; after all, it would be foolish to rely upon a surgeon who picked up their scalpel skills on YouTube. Nor would we trust an IT professional to fix a leaking water heater.

Specialization is an essential path that people should pursue diligently. However, it's equally vital to remember that expertise in one domain should not restrict our perspectives.

I encourage you to tread multiple lanes, acknowledging that while one lane may be highly specialized, the other lanes contribute to a more comprehensive view of the world. In my view, it is the collaboration of generalists and specialists, working side-by-side, that will create a more prepared future.

If you're a surgeon, I encourage you to pick up a paintbrush and try your hands at art. If you're an artist, I encourage you to pick up a hammer and try your skills at woodworking. If you're a carpenter, I encourage you to consider looking at engineering courses at a local college. Expand your life beyond your comfort zone.

Once you've tried a new lane, I hope you choose another and another until you're living in multiple lanes and feeling the excitement of doing multiple things each and every day. Simply put, I want you to open your mind, your hands, and your whole self to being more than you are today.

But let's shift our focus to the tangible experiences that have shaped my path toward becoming a true advocate for this transformative approach, filled with twists, turns, and invaluable lessons learned along the way.

Did You Stop Wanting to Be More?

I am someone who once made the mistake of thinking I could stay in one lane. But at the same time, I can assure you that *learning* new things was never something I actively sought. It wasn't about learning. It was about *not knowing*.

As fate would have it, my journey of learning came about in response to a hyperactive curiosity. I did want to know everything and do everything! *I wanted to be more!*

Maybe it was some form of professional ADD or a reaction to boredom, but I always seemed to find something that caught my interest and became a new obsession. I have never been without this drive, but I remember how much I panicked when I had to *learn something in school. I* also used to worry about how much time something would take to learn. As we will discuss later, the art of learning was something I would master to feed my ravenous curiosity.

It was through a series of unexpected events that I found myself expanding my horizons and embracing new opportunities for growth and development.

I was always known as the kid who did well in school. I seemed to have a natural aptitude for learning, excelling in most subjects without much effort. However, there was a catch: I hated studying. The idea of sitting down and poring over textbooks for hours on end made me cringe, but my desire to learn and understand was an energy that knew no bounds.

The notion of becoming a specialist, or of dedicating my entire life to the study of a single topic, was as unfamiliar to me as the distant stars. While many, including my parents and high school guidance counselors, fervently advocated for specialization, pointing me toward the holy grail of being a lawyer, I couldn't help but draw from the excitement of my grandfather's experiences and beliefs. He, too, had embraced the multifaceted world of multidisciplinarity, and his guidance had a profound impact on my perspective. To me, being a specialist was never the answer, and I held steadfast to that conviction.

Growing up, you might also have been a person who was interested in various areas. If so, the desire to become a generalist or to explore multiple disciplines was likely born within you. The idea of being a specialist or spending your life studying one topic might have felt foreign, and you might have questioned the conventional wisdom that pushed you in that direction. You may have observed the power of multidisciplinary thinking in your own life, even if it was in subtle ways. Perhaps you've encountered situations where your ability to connect ideas from different fields gave you an advantage. Your journey towards multidisciplinarity might have started with small steps, much like mine did. But, in the grand scheme, like me, you probably followed the safe path of a more focused, specialized career.

My Multidisciplinary Journey

This book is a result of my life's journey. As you read this book, I hope that you will reach into your own heart and soul and find your own distinct multidisciplinary journey. Whether it's something you lived outwardly or something that you buried to be a specialist, I hope it comes to the forefront and flourishes.

I first observed the power of multidisciplinary thinking when I went to a construction site with my father. As a child I would watch him work with architects, engineers, electricians, cabinet makers, and all the trades on a commercial project. Every one of them spoke a different language. Every one of them had ideas. And every single one of them knew that they were right. They thought everyone else was wrong.

My father was always the one who brought them all to the table to hear their concerns and ideas and find a way to make it work. You see, architects design things. Engineers make sure they stay standing and that the mechanics function properly. The construction trades are the ones in the field who have to merge the ideas of the architects and engineers to make their pipe dreams a reality. I spent many days watching my father talk and discuss technical problems with people only to flesh out those specific areas where their individual geniuses crossed paths.

My father was an expert at finding the intersection between disciplines to make everything happen. I was amazed by his ability to get things done. Sometimes he screamed, but more often than not he did it with socialization and finesse, a union carpenter with the skills to see the details that the specialist could not. I always thought my father knew enough about all of the trades and all of the engineering and all of the design work to be dangerous.

Those formative days watching my father navigate this intricate web of expertise left an indelible mark on my understanding of how multidisciplinary collaboration could truly shine. Amidst this symphony of diverse perspectives, my father assumed the role of both conductor and diplomat, orchestrating conversations that transformed technical problems into opportunities for collective genius to flourish. It was in watching him work that I first saw the raw power of cross-disciplinary thinking in action.

I always wanted to know a little bit about everything so I could be more like him, but he always insisted that I had to be *better* than him. So, unfortunately, he sent me on a journey to learn more. In his mind he wanted me to be a specialist in engineering or he wanted me to be a lawyer. He never imagined that I would want to know a little bit about everything. Right from that pivotal moment with my dad, everything we're about to unravel in this book began to take shape.

The Many Paths We Walk

Embracing a variety of experiences often reveals valuable lessons that a singular path might overlook. When I was a Boy Scout, every merit badge represented not just a skill, but a lesson in curiosity and perseverance. They were more than accolades; they were symbols of a hunger to know and explore. When it came time to apply these skills in the classroom, I found I was able to learn more effectively and efficiently.

Upon entering Temple University College of Engineering Technology, despite being aimed towards engineering, my gaze often wandered towards other disciplines. I questioned the conventional wisdom that urged specialization. Why? Because even in a field as exacting as engineering, I believed there was wisdom to be gleaned from philosophy and the arts. By challenging the norms and integrating philosophy courses into my engineering curriculum, I learned that true education is about *bridging seemingly disparate domains.*

I pretty much had FOMO before anybody knew what FOMO was. I always had a fear of missing out on what everyone else was doing.

The introduction of computers in the 80s highlighted another lesson: *adaptability.* While my peers struggled to evolve with technology, my varied background allowed me to embrace it. I knew it wasn't just about understanding code but understanding its broader implications in our world.

Even during the rigors of education at Temple University School of Law, my quest to learn in other lanes didn't wane. My proactive decision to take a typing course against mainstream advice accidentally positioned me ahead on the digital curve, underscoring the importance of foresight and initiative. (Yes, advisors told me I didn't need typing because there would "always be someone in the office to type for me.")

Years later, as professionals scrambled to adjust to technological advances, the real lesson came into focus. Success isn't merely about expertise in a chosen field. It's about agility, continual learning, and recognizing the interplay between diverse disciplines. My diverse experiences weren't just paths taken; they were lessons learned and life skills acquired. And these lessons tell us that in an ever-evolving world, a multidisciplinary approach isn't just beneficial—it's essential.

Focus on Your Path

As we dive deeper into this book, remember that your journey is the heart of our exploration. The principles and insights we'll uncover are meant to empower and encourage you to further embrace and benefit from your multidisciplinary mindset. Your path may be unique, but the potential for growth, creativity, and fulfillment through multidisciplinarity is something we can all aspire to achieve. As we traverse the ever-evolving landscapes of learning and professional endeavors, a multidisciplinary approach isn't merely a choice—it's a necessity for holistic growth, adaptability, and success. Let this journey inspire you to unlock your full potential by continuously seeking knowledge, understanding, and mastery across diverse fields.

I'm excited to have you along on this journey as I entice you to embrace a multidisciplinary life. Whether you're a student, a professional, or simply someone who is curious about the world, there is always something new to learn and discover. By approaching life with an open mind and a willingness to explore, you can unlock your full potential and create a rich, fulfilling, and meaningful life.

What Are Journey Mileposts?

At the end of each chapter, a section like the one below named *JOURNEY MILEPOSTS* will provide a roadside stop on our journey. Just like when you're traveling on vacation, you'll reflect on where you've been, but you'll also think ahead and dream about where you're going. You may not have all the answers when we reach a milepost, but you can imagine. Some of the answers will become more obvious as you go on, but I encourage you to anticipate the destination as you read this book. Allow all of your life experience in learning to surface and empower you. That is your multidisciplinary nature.

JOURNEY MILEPOSTS

- **Exploring Your Multidisciplinary Life:** Have you ever considered expanding your skill set beyond your current profession? Reflect on the advantages of blending skills and knowledge from different fields. How could a multidisciplinary approach reshape the way you tackle challenges?

- **Adaptability and Broadened Perspectives:** In today's ever-changing world, how do you keep up? Consider the value of adaptability and the power of seeing things from multiple angles. Can enhancing your adaptability make you more receptive to new opportunities and ideas?

- **Career Opportunities and Personal Growth:** Think about your current career or hobbies. How might introducing knowledge or techniques from another discipline enhance your performance or enjoyment? Are there unexplored avenues that could potentially amplify your current endeavors?

- **Embracing the Role of a Generalist:** The term *generalist* is often misunderstood. Reflect on its true essence: not as a jack-of-all-trades, but as a master of integration. How can being a generalist, capable of linking diverse ideas, position you as a valuable asset in any team or project? We will talk more later about the jack-of-all-trades label, but for now begin to think of it as a positive.

- **Specialization vs. Multidisciplinarity:** Specialization is undoubtedly valuable, but have you considered its limitations? Ponder the benefits of collaborating with specialists while maintaining a generalist's broad perspective. Could this balance lead to more comprehensive solutions and richer experiences?

- **Your Personal Multidisciplinary Journey:** Take a moment to chart your own learning journey. Are there interests or passions you've left unexplored? Recall instances where a diverse skill set or knowledge might have benefited you. What steps can you take today to begin or further your multidisciplinary journey?

SEE MORE

2

Widening the Lens: a Grandfather, a Puppet, and a Poet

*Do I contradict myself? Very well, then I contradict myself,
I am large, I contain multitudes.*
— Walt Whitman, *Song of Myself*

On a typical Wednesday morning, as I observed Emily, who had a strong background in finance, meticulously comb through a financial report, I was struck by her commitment to detail, ensuring every discrepancy was addressed. However, stepping back, I noticed something more pervasive, not just in this room or with Emily, but a pattern in many workplaces and societal structures. It wasn't a reflection of Emily's competence but a broader realization of what I've termed *Strategic Tunnel Vision*, or *STV*.

This myopic view of the world isn't confined to corner offices and boardrooms. It's a societal tendency that manifests when individuals, focused on a particular field or expertise, inadvertently overlook the broader picture. Consider the tech aficionado, always chasing the next big innovation but oblivious to the human element, or the proficient analyst, lost in numbers, missing out on the human stories they tell.

This restrictive view isn't new, but the good news is that there's a way out: *Embrace diverse perspectives and cross-disciplinary thinking*. Here are some teasers to widen the lens...

The Panorama of Possibilities

Look Beyond the Obvious: Engaging in dialogues beyond your main expertise brings a fresh perspective. It offers a wider view, revealing overlooked facets.

Craft with Care: A range of insights and decisions, whether in business or daily life, helps you become more holistic. It's like painting with a myriad of colors, each one adding depth and dimension.

The Magic of Collaboration: The most revolutionary ideas often arise from a melting pot of thoughts. When you combine the flair of a creative with the precision of a technician you get something unique and powerful.

Hidden Hazards: Just as one might see an impending storm but miss the rocks beneath, in life and in business we face both obvious and concealed challenges. A broad-minded approach prepares you for both.

Echoing Across Ecosystems: Whether it's a business or a community, there's a network of interdependencies. Adopting a versatile strategy ensures coherence and balance.

While there's undeniable value in specialization, the magic truly happens when we bridge the gaps, letting diverse streams of thought flow into one another. For the leaders of today, shaking off the confines of STV is more than just a strategy—it's the heart of enduring success. So, here's to viewing our world through a mosaic of lenses, engaging in rich, varied dialogues, and crafting strategies that resonate with every soul involved.

Adopting multidisciplinary thinking can dramatically enrich your life, ushering in an era of boundless curiosity and exploration. By transcending the boundaries of specialized fields and weaving insights from diverse domains, you will not only broaden your intellectual horizons but also cultivate more profound empathy and understanding of the world around you.

Living with such a mindset means every day is an opportunity for discovery, every interaction a lesson, and every challenge a multidimensional puzzle waiting to be solved. Ultimately, embracing a multidisciplinary life allows one to live in a world brimming with excitement, wonder, and fulfillment. Yes, this is the raw power of cross-disciplinary thinking.

Life isn't merely about the roles we play in professional settings, but the myriad shades of experiences, stories, and passions that define us. It's this intricate dance between diverse experiences and learnings that shape us, as it shaped me.

The journey of multidisciplinarity isn't any ordinary path—it's an exhilarating adventure of perpetual growth, where each day presents an opportunity to evolve, to be a shade brighter and bolder than the day before.

The Grandfather

The tapestry of my inspirations is woven from both the familiar threads of the mainstream and the intricate patterns of the unexpected. Let's dive into a story that starts with a voice many in old-school Philadelphia would recognize.

Imagine a man who oversaw the grandeur of Philadelphia's public property by day and captivated the radio airwaves by night. That man was my grandfather.

By day, he oversaw all the property that the city of Philadelphia owned. (And yes, that included the Liberty Bell.) He was a developer, an architect, a designer, and a master storyteller. From managing facilities, maintenance schedules, capital projects, or land acquisitions to the human relations component of overseeing all the departments' employees, he had a broad range of diverse responsibilities. He was a master of hard and soft skill management.

Well organized and technically proficient, he had a personality that made everyone in Philadelphia City Hall love him. In my younger years, when I got on the elevator at City Hall, the elevator operator and everyone in the elevator knew him and made sure that I was safely escorted to his office.

But when the nights and weekends arrived, he was the charismatic Sherry O'Brien, a pioneer of sports radio to listeners on WDAS radio during the golden age of the '40s and '50s. Born Charles Augustus Ignatius Sheridan, he legally changed his name to Sherry O'Brien and that was how the people of Philadelphia knew this warm-hearted and very interesting giant of a man. His name and identity were the full person he was intended to be.

Today, in an age when everything is available on our cell phones, I must share that my grandfather was a sports announcer in a time of far more primitive technology. There were no computers in the studio, no iPads in the announcer's booth, and no way to pull up information on the phone. He was a man alone with a microphone and the thoughts in his head. Every batting average, every boxing bout, and every race car driver's wins and losses were in his head. He knew everything about sports and shared it with his audience, ad libbing and painting the airways with words.

From the echo of his voice, tales of legendary sports figures like Connie Mack, Rocky Marciano, and Jesse Owens came alive. Beyond the radio and his management role at City Hall, my grandfather was a scratch golfer, a trained architect, and a passionate announcer at vibrant live events, ranging from wrestling bouts to thrilling Major League Baseball games at the old Shibe Park, later known as Connie Mack Stadium.

One of his most cherished friendships was with Connie Mack, the iconic baseball catcher, legendary manager, and team owner. Through this bond, my childhood was illuminated with mesmerizing tales of Philadelphia sporting's golden era.

Yet beyond his many titles, my grandfather was an unparalleled storyteller. His myriad interests and vast knowledge made Saturday mornings at Langhorne Speedway an exhilarating experience, introducing a young me to racing legends like A.J. Foyt and Mario Andretti.

With every curious inquiry I pitched, he responded with wisdom and patience. He wasn't just sharing information; he was nurturing a young mind's thirst for knowledge. Through him I glimpsed the embodiment of a true multidisciplinary expert.

Every time I reflected on his tales and wisdom, one thought prevailed: *I aspire to possess the breadth and depth of knowledge he does.* And so, my journey began.

The Puppet

The more peculiar source of my inspiration was Jerry Mahoney, a ventriloquism dummy that was given life, not just by the magic of puppetry, but by the sheer brilliance of its operator, Paul Winchell.

As a child, I sat riveted every time Jerry and Winchell appeared on the television, whether on glitzy variety shows, profound talk shows, or during their special moments on the *Winchell-Mahoney Time* show. However, it wasn't just Jerry who held my gaze; it was the mesmerizing aura of Paul Winchell. He wasn't simply an entertainer; he was an enchanter. The line between the puppet and the puppeteer, reality and fantasy, seemed indistinguishably blurred when Winchell took the stage.

But the tale of Winchell doesn't end at ventriloquism. As his entertainment career evolved, he breathed life into one of our beloved childhood characters, lending his voice to the exuberant Tigger in Disney's *Winnie the Pooh*. With every

"Hoo-hoo-hoo!" Winchell's vivacity became palpable, turning ink-and-paint sketches into a spirited tiger.

Inspired by him, I yearned to be a ventriloquist. My parents, supporting my newfound curiosity, gifted me a Danny O'Day ventriloquism doll. It was during these earnest but fumbling attempts that I discovered my lips weren't adept at deceit. Thus, my short-lived dream was hindered by my inability to speak without moving my lips, leading me instead to the world of magic, where articulation had a different meaning. But let's save that story for another day.

Winchell's entertainment world, vast as it is, was just a chapter in the fascinating book of his life. His narrative is punctuated with more than just entertainment feats. Deeply fascinated by the intricate mechanics of ventriloquism, he innovated beyond the stage, living in multiple lanes, truly multidisciplinary.

Winchell attended Columbia with the intent to go on to medical school. Unfortunately, family finances didn't allow that, but his fascination with the world of medicine did not leave his soul. His crowning achievement branched from an unexpected blend of his pre-med education and entertainment experience. Like all true visionaries, Winchell recognized the boundaries of his own expertise, so in a masterstroke of collaboration, he enlisted the help of Dr. Henry Heimlich (yes, the very name we associate with that life-saving maneuver), creating a fusion of artistic flair with the meticulous precision of science. Winchell applied his knowledge of mechanics, gleaned from the inner workings of a ventriloquist's dummy, and his budding medical curiosity, to conceptualize and patent, along with Dr. Heimlich, the first human artificial heart. This remarkable invention was generously donated to the University of Utah, paving the way for the Jarvik-7, a precursor to today's heart replacements.

With over 30 patents, his name linked to everyday marvels like disposable razor blades and flameless cigarette lighters, it's easy to paint Winchell as a master inventor, but in a world brimming with tales of unexpected alliances, few are as intriguing as the merging of ventriloquism with medical innovation. It's a blend that raises eyebrows, prompts smiles of incredulity, and perhaps even elicits a chuckle or two. But within this curious intersection of disciplines lies Winchell's story—a narrative that challenges us to reimagine the vast expanse of human potential.

Yet, Winchell was not just an inventor or an artist; he was a treasure trove of multifaceted interests. His intellectual hunger paints the portrait of a true multidisciplinary mind. His life was a testament to a spirit that refused confinement, that constantly sought the thrill of the unknown, agile, adaptable, resilient, and driven by lifelong learning.

The spotlight that followed Winchell didn't just bathe him in its glow; it illuminated the breadth of his endeavors, turning his fame into a torch that showcased the sheer diversity of his passions. In the story of Winchell, we witness the symphony of multidimensionality. He provides a poignant testament that life is vast, varied, and unboxed.

As my childhood years waned, I continued with my education. It was at Temple University College of Engineering that I received my Bachelor of Science in Engineering Technology, and it was at the Temple University law school that I received my law degree. Like many of you, I pursued the prescribed path. Sure, I studied engineering before law, which was unheard of, but I followed the route of specialization, just as everyone said that I should. And yet, I was haunted by thoughts of my grandfather, of Paul Winchell, and of others whom I saw as multidisciplinary, so I wandered off into tangents on a regular basis, learning and perfecting something here, then moving on to another area to learn something new there.

My life was a constant array of learning and of asking myself, *What new thing did I learn today?* Even when I was in law school, when other students sought jobs in law offices, I worked on high steel, walking on six-inch beams far above the city of Philadelphia. I could see City Hall, Independence Hall, Carpenters Hall and, of course, the Ben Franklin Bridge, and especially the magnificent Walt Whitman Bridge. I toiled in its shadow, oblivious to the profound connection between this colossal structure and the enigmatic poet who inspired its name.

The Poet

Walt Whitman, born in 1819 on Long Island, was destined to become an emblematic figure in American literature. His life, like the city around me, was a testament to diversity and complexity. He began as a humble printer's apprentice, later tried his hand at journalism, taught school, and even worked as a government clerk. He was, in essence, a multidisciplinary soul, a man who defied categorization.

It was through his poetry that Whitman's multidisciplinary nature shone brightest. His magnum opus, *Leaves of Grass*, wasn't just a collection of verses; it was a manifestation of his multitudes. His words celebrated the individual and the collective, the common and the extraordinary, the self and the universe.

In those pages, I discovered a man who dared to declare, "I celebrate myself, and sing myself." But Whitman wasn't just singing himself; he was singing the collective soul of America. He traversed the continent, from the bustling streets of New York City to the untamed expanses of the West, capturing the spirit of a rapidly changing nation in his verses.

As I wandered the streets of Philadelphia, I couldn't help but see the echoes of Whitman's multitudes all around me. The city was a patchwork of cultures, each contributing to its rich tapestry. From the historic sites like Independence Hall to vibrant neighborhoods like South Philly, the city embodied the diverse spirit that Whitman had celebrated.

It was beneath the Walt Whitman Bridge, on a brisk autumn evening, that I felt the convergence of my own multitudes. The bridge, with its colossal steel arches, seemed to span the gap between my past and present, between the me I once was and the me I was becoming.

In that moment I realized that I, too, was a product of multitudes. I had grown up in a city that embraced diversity and complexity, just as Whitman had. The bridge became a symbol of connection, a physical representation of Whitman's call to embrace the myriad facets of our own existence.

As I stood there, gazing up at the bridge's towering form, I couldn't help but think of the reader, the one who might stumble upon this chapter in a book. I am glad you are joining me on this journey of exploration, to embrace the multidisciplinary nature of life, and to discover the multitudes within yourself. Just as Walt Whitman found unity in his diverse experiences and celebrated the complexity of the human spirit, so too can we embark on a journey to become multitudes. In a world that often seeks to define us in narrow terms, let us heed Whitman's call and revel in the richness of our own existence. Together, we can celebrate the multitudes within us, beneath the timeless shadow of the Walt Whitman Bridge and beyond.

In the early chapters of my life, the stories of two remarkable men, my grandfather and Paul Winchell, ignited the spark of multidisciplinarity within me. My grandfather, with his resplendent tales from Philadelphia's golden era and his innate ability to wear many hats, taught me the beauty of mastering diverse skills. Winchell, the dazzling ventriloquist and innovator, expanded my horizons, showing me that a singular passion can lead to many roads, each as rewarding as the other. Their stories weren't just tales of their times but guiding lighthouses for a young dreamer.

As I sat many years ago, absorbing the brilliance of my grandfather, an aspiration was kindled within me, a longing to tread diverse paths and embrace the magic that ensues when seemingly unrelated worlds converge. Whitman showcased a life unbounded by labels, one that thrived on continuous learning, and it is his legacy that fueled my desires to venture into the vast mosaic of a life lived in a multitude of lanes.

And like many of you, I didn't even realize the vast number of lanes I lived in until a very dear friend pointed out the uniqueness of my own life. Everything that I ever did was incorporated, seamlessly, into everything I do now and all that I would ever do. It's this magical intertwining of lanes that makes a multidisciplinary life exciting and fruitful.

Through this tale, I extend an invitation to you: to revel in the brilliance of diverse passions and to embark on a journey to discover the magical destinations to which they can guide us. But now, as I reflect upon the remarkable lives of my grandfather and Paul Winchell, and the poetic multitudes of Walt Whitman, I can't help but be inspired by the vibrant array of their experiences. Their stories serve as poignant reminders that life is a rich mosaic of diverse interests and talents, waiting to be explored and celebrated.

Just as I once watched Emily's laser focus, I now stand ready to embrace the exhilarating adventure of multidisciplinarity. With each step, I aim to be a shade brighter and bolder than the day before, weaving my own story into the ever-expanding panorama of possibilities.

So let us embark together on this journey, where the intersection of diverse passions illuminates the path to untold destinations, and where the multitudes within us await discovery.

JOURNEY MILEPOSTS

- **Strategic Tunnel Vision:** I have introduced you to my concept of STV, where individuals focused on their expertise tend to overlook the broader picture. Have you ever experienced or observed this phenomenon in your workplace or personal life? How did it impact the outcomes?

- **Embracing Diverse Perspectives:** Embracing diverse perspectives and multidisciplinary thinking can help overcome tunnel vision. Can you think of examples where diverse perspectives led to innovative solutions or breakthroughs? How can you encourage diverse thinking in your own life or work?

- **The Power of Collaboration:** We discussed collaboration between individuals with different backgrounds and expertise to highlight a source of revolutionary ideas. Can you recall instances where collaboration played a significant role in achieving success, whether in your career, projects, or personal life?

- **Recognizing Hidden Hazards:** Consider the importance of being prepared for both obvious and concealed challenges. How can a broad-minded approach help to identify and address hidden hazards in various aspects of life or business?

- **Multidisciplinary Inspiration:** I shared my personal stories of individuals like my grandfather, Paul Winchell, and Walt Whitman, who embodied multidisciplinarity. Have you encountered multidisciplinary role models in your life? How have they influenced your perspective on learning and exploration?

- **Personal Multidisciplinarity:** My journey into multidisciplinarity was an adventure of perpetual growth. I tell my story because I know many people, including you, who have walked in multiple lanes without embracing them. Have you ever considered pursuing diverse interests or skills outside your primary field of expertise? How might such exploration enrich your life and experiences?

3

The Integrated Mindset: Thinking in Multiple Lanes

> *Many men go fishing all of their lives without knowing that it is not fish they are after.*
> — Henry David Thoreau

We are all multitudes. Each of us possesses a personality of infinite facets. What do we do with our multifaceted nature? Many of us keep our blinders on and move forward without becoming all that we should be. Yes, we've been told to pick a lane. we've been told specialize. Some of us find this comforting, but some of us feel like caged animals because there's so much more out there, just beyond our reach.

The notion of containing multitudes is liberating. It allows us to be more accepting of ourselves and others, recognizing that we all have unique experiences, perspectives, and identities. It allows us to take off the blinders and to get out of the lane we've picked. It encourages us to celebrate the richness and diversity of human life.

Being multidisciplinary is a game-changer. It helps us stand out from the crowd, adapt to changing environments, and open doors to new and exciting opportunities. To be multidisciplinary is to constantly challenge yourself and explore new ideas.

Think about a multidisciplinary medical team, where radiologists, cardiologists, dermatologists, and other specialists collaborate to provide treatment. The more multidisciplinary you become, the more you acquire new knowledge and new skills, the more you will naturally begin to see where disciplines cross paths. The multidisciplinary person understands which specialists and experts need to work together to accomplish any task. This awareness is the special province of the multidisciplinary person. It isn't available to the specialist. As you grow and develop your portfolio of disciplines, you'll be drawn to other fields because you'll see the intersections before you take the leap.

In multidisciplinary teams, all of the disciplines sit around a table and come up with a plan, and people who are multi-disciplined always bring something to the table. In the Information Age it's become increasingly clear that the days of the specialist-only mindset are numbered. We can no longer rely on a single area of expertise to solve the complex problems we face. We need people who can navigate and make sense of the diverse and ever-changing landscape of knowledge. We need generalists.

The Generalist's Path to Enlightenment

Generalist has often been a negative term, describing someone who knows a little about a lot but not much about anything, lacking the depth of understanding to solve complex problems. However, in today's world, the generalist is an increasingly valuable and necessary player. As we begin our journey, I want to make it clear that being a generalist does not require a deep dive into any one field. Each discipline that you learn will be focused, but the depth of knowledge will have boundaries. Being a generalist is about choosing a level of expertise and limiting your depth of knowledge within a given domain. If it sounds like you're undercutting yourself, remember: What you sacrifice in depth you will make up for in breadth. By learning to think wider, you will discover more crossroads of knowledge, more ways to integrate what you know into any situation, and *that* is where great things will happen.

Being multidisciplinary creates the ability to think across silos and in multiple lanes simultaneously. It's about increasing your ability to think, problem-solve, and explore those magical places that a specialist will miss.

Action

Becoming multidisciplinary is about more than just learning. It's about *taking action* on what you know. It's about *living*, not just *thinking*, in multiple lanes. As we'll see, having skin in the game is not optional. You cannot gain knowledge of all the nuances unless you get in the mud and get dirty.

If you're going to study art, get some paint on your hands. If you're going to study woodworking, drive some nails. If you're going to study engineering, go stand in some wet cement and see how long it takes to harden. Only when you actually do something with your newfound skills will you become enlightened to the path of the generalist. Only then will you find the intersections that everyone else overlooks.

Plato and the Polymaths

Polymathy, or the ability to master multiple disciplines, has been praised and revered since the time of the ancient Greeks. Today, more than ever, we should appreciate the value of polymathy and its potential to enhance creativity, problem-solving, and innovation, yet modern society has largely rejected it in favor of narrow specialization, with education systems and workplaces emphasizing singular pursuits and compartmentalization. This is a mistake. We need generalists to help us navigate the complex and rapidly changing world of the 21st century.

One the oldest written works that encourages diversified learning is Plato's *The Republic* which argues that education is a crucial component of creating a just society and that it should be diverse and multifaceted. Plato believed that education should not be limited to one discipline or area of study, but should encompass a wide range of subjects, including music, mathematics, astronomy, and philosophy. He also emphasized the importance of physical education and the development of the whole person. One of the book's most celebrated passages is the Allegory of the Cave, a powerful metaphor that explores the nature of reality and the role of education and enlightenment in human understanding. Plato describes a group of people who are confined in a cave, chained to a wall, and unable to turn their heads. Behind them, unseen, a fire burns, casting shadows on the opposite wall that the prisoners mistake for reality. One of the prisoners is eventually freed and brought outside the cave where he discovers the true nature of reality and the world beyond the shadows.

Plato's allegory is a warning against relying solely on our senses and our limited perception of reality. It also emphasizes the importance of education and critical thinking in unlocking a deeper understanding of the world. In a sense, failing to broaden our perspective beyond our own narrow viewpoint and knowledge base makes us little better than those prisoners chained to a wall, ignorant of the expansive world beyond their darkened cave.

Plato's remedy is diversified learning, suggesting that we need to explore different perspectives and experiences to fully understand the world around us, to challenge our own beliefs, and to seek out new knowledge and a well-rounded education that encompasses a diverse range of subjects.

Both the multidisciplinary thinker and the polymath have a wide range of knowledge and experience. However, their journeys are distinctly different. A multidisciplinary thinker is not someone who studies deeply in multiple disciplines. That is left to the polymath.

A multidisciplinary thinker focuses on achieving integrated insights from various disciplines and valuing the cross pollination of ideas to become more holistic in their approach to everything. So, diversify your learning, go deep in some areas, but then go broad.

Focus your efforts on becoming adaptable, agile, and adept at utilizing knowledge from a broad range of domains to weave everything that you know together into a new you to enhance your life, business, and goals.

The Parable of the Elephant

Our approach to the world—and the limitations of perspective—are well illustrated by the Parable of the Elephant: Three blind people encounter an elephant for the first time. Relying solely on touch, each person grasps a different part of the creature to understand its nature. The one touching the trunk confidently claims that it is like a hose. Another, feeling a leg, insists it's akin to a tree. The third, holding the tail, declares it to be a rope. Their individual perspectives, confined to their immediate experiences, lead them to three different and somewhat conflicting conclusions.

The story, at its core, is about partial understanding and the pitfalls of limited perspectives, phenomena prevalent in today's specialized world. In academia, business, or even in daily life, we often get ensnared in our niche, believing our slice of expertise gives us a comprehensive understanding.

But much like the blind people, this can result in a skewed perception. While specialization has its merits, a solely myopic view often leads to misinterpretations or oversights. Even in our own thinking we do not always allow our individual lanes to communicate and integrate. This is where the power of a wider view comes into play. Imagine if the blind people had combined their experiences and communicated effectively. Their collective understanding of the elephant would have been richer and more accurate.

Similarly, a decision based in multiple disciplines—say, economics, psychology, and history—is likely to be more robust than one shaped by a narrow focus. By fusing our individual lanes, like the logic of our mathematician lane with the creative insights of our artistic hobby lane, we can achieve solutions that are both innovative and practical.

As a Man Thinketh in His Heart So Is He

During my early years of legal practice, a friend of mine, Charlie "Tremendous" Jones, handed me a copy of James Allen's classic book *As a Man Thinketh*. Despite being published in 1902, this book is still widely read because its central message is timeless and universal, emphasizing the power of our minds and how it shapes our lives. It encourages readers to take control of their thoughts and use them to create the lives they desire.

In today's world, so filled with negativity, stress, and uncertainty, the message of *As a Man Thinketh* is more important than ever. Many of us struggle with negative thinking patterns that hold us back from achieving our goals and living fulfilling lives. In addition to everything else I've mentioned,

As a Man Thinketh provides a roadmap for overcoming those patterns and cultivating a more positive and productive mindset.

More importantly, in a world where many of us feel helpless or powerless in the face of external circumstances, such as pandemics and political turmoil, *As a Man Thinketh* emphasizes the importance of taking responsibility for one's own life and actions. It's an important idea to remember and it's one we'll come back to: We always have the power to control our thoughts and actions, even in difficult situations, and there's no better way to do that than by controlling our learning. The more you seek to better yourself by practicing in new and inventive lanes, the more empowered and happier you'll be.

Since I'm throwing old books at you, let's also mention Thomas Paine's *Common Sense* which advocates the idea that we should use our own common sense to make decisions rather than relying on tradition, authority, or popular opinion. It encourages individuals to seek out knowledge and expertise from a variety of fields and perspectives in order to make informed decisions. When you take a multidisciplinary approach to life you will develop your own common sense and critical thinking skills, helping you navigate complex issues and make sound decisions.

Being multidisciplinary is being prepared for change. It's exploring and learning about a variety of subjects, from science to art, technology to philosophy, and beyond. The multidisciplinary life opens you up to new ideas, new perspectives, and new ways of thinking. It's a constant intersection of multiple fields and perspectives. It brings a sense of fulfillment and purpose. It lets you discover new talents and find meaning in unexpected places. You may even find that your diverse experiences and knowledge come together to create a unique and fulfilling career path that you couldn't have imagined without the multidisciplinary approach.

Embracing a multidisciplinary life requires a willingness to step outside your comfort zone and challenge yourself to learn and grow in new ways. But the rewards of such an approach are immeasurable. You will develop a more nuanced understanding of the world and your place in it, and you will discover new passions and interests that you never knew existed.

By the end of this book, you will have a deeper understanding of the multidisciplinary approach to learning and problem-solving, and the skills and mindset required to become an effective generalist. You will have the tools to build networks across disciplines, communicate effectively, and take action based on your newfound multidisciplinary experience and knowledge.

You will hold the key to a way of life that promises limitless horizons and greater opportunities than you ever dreamed were possible.

JOURNEY MILEPOSTS

- **Embracing Our Multifaceted Nature:** Reflect on your own multifaceted nature. How can you better acknowledge and nurture the various facets of your personality and interests?

- **The Power of Multidisciplinarity:** Explore the benefits of being multidisciplinary. How might it enhance your ability to adapt to change and seize new opportunities in your life and career.

- **The Need for Generalists:** Consider the role of generalists in solving complex problems and navigating the ever-changing landscape of knowledge. Even before you get into the meat of this book, ask yourself, *What qualities make a successful generalist, and how might I develop them?*

- **Balancing Depth and Breadth:** Reflect on the concept of choosing a level of expertise with boundaries in various domains. How comfortable are you with sacrificing depth for breadth in your pursuits, and what advantages can a broader perspective bring to your life and work?

- **Taking Action and Gaining Experience:** Think about the importance of taking action and gaining hands-on experience in multiple disciplines. How do you approach learning by doing, and how has it shaped your understanding of different areas of knowledge?

- **Cultivating a Positive Mindset:** Explore the role of mindset in shaping your life. How can you apply the principles of positive thinking and take control of your thoughts and actions to enhance your well-being and personal growth?

4

The Map: Becoming a Generalist

*If you skillfully follow the multidisciplinary path,
you will never wish to come back. It would be
like cutting off your hands.*
— Charlie Munger

Would you like to be happy and successful? Most of us would, but it isn't always easy. If you want to get ahead and use your time and energy to advance yourself along the road of life instead of simply treading water, cultivating multidisciplinary knowledge, skills, and expertise will help get you there.

Success and Happiness in Four Simple Steps

1. **Identify Your Interests and Strengths:** The first step on the multidisciplinary path to success and happiness is to identify your interests and strengths. One way or

another, you've been doing this most of your life. Now is the time to do it consciously. Explore different fields and disciplines to discover what you're passionate about. Once you've identified your interests and strengths, begin developing your skills in those areas.

It's also essential to be open to new ideas and experiences. Don't limit yourself to a particular field but instead explore every area that interests you. Being a generalist allows you to connect different fields and create unique solutions to problems.

2. **Set Priorities:** The second step to achieving success and happiness is to set priorities that align with your personal values and strengths. Some things you may wish to accomplish immediately; others, while still important, may take years to achieve. It's also important to break your goals into smaller, more manageable tasks. The first stage of writing a bestseller isn't to call an agent, it's to put your hands on a keyboard and start typing. This piecemeal approach of smaller subtasks makes your larger goals more achievable and helps you track your progress.

3. **Manage Your Time and Resources:** The third step to achieving success and happiness is to manage your time and resources effectively. Time is a finite resource, and it's essential to use it wisely to achieve your goals. Effective time management involves

prioritizing tasks, delegating responsibilities, and avoiding distractions.

Effective resource management requires a clear understanding of your financial and physical resources. You should develop a budget to manage your finances and ensure that you're allocating your resources appropriately. You should also track your progress regularly and make adjustments as needed.

4. **Cultivate Resilience and a Growth Mindset:** The final step to achieving success and happiness is to cultivate resilience and a growth mindset. Resilience is the ability to recover quickly from setbacks and adversity. A growth mindset is the belief that your abilities and intelligence can be developed through hard work and dedication. Cultivating a growth mindset means embracing challenges and viewing them as opportunities for growth, being open to feedback, and using it to improve yourself. To develop resilience, focus on the positive aspects of a situation, practice self-care, and seek support from others.

You'll notice I didn't spend a lot of time—only a couple of paragraphs each—on any one of those four steps. Each one is a whole self-improvement category unto itself, and each is foundational and fairly basic. They provide the bottom floor of our multidisciplinary pyramid, so if you need help setting goals, cultivating a growth mindset, etc., there are whole libraries available to help you do those things. What you won't find whole libraries devoted to is becoming multidisciplinary. So get those four steps in order, get help if you need it, and let's continue our 30,000-foot tour of becoming a solid generalist.

Building a Multidisciplinary Mindset

Building a multidisciplinary mindset is a process that requires deliberate and continuous efforts. Here are some ways to develop a multidisciplinary mindset:

Expose Yourself to Different Fields: It's essential to expose yourself to different fields and subjects outside your areas of expertise. Reading books, attending seminars, watching documentaries, and taking online courses are all great, and even fun, ways of doing this. This exposure will help you develop an understanding of different perspectives and ways of thinking that the single-lane life can't provide.

Network: Networking with people from different fields will help you gain new insights and knowledge. Attend conferences and events related to your new areas of interest, even a few that are completely foreign to you, and cultivate relationships with experts from these areas.

Collaborate: Working with people from different backgrounds and disciplines can help you learn new approaches and perspectives. Collaborating with others can expand your mind and lead to innovative solutions that would not have been possible otherwise.

Learn Continuously: Adopt a mindset of lifelong learning. Keep yourself updated with the latest trends and advancements in your areas of expertise, and also in other fields. This will help you stay relevant and adapt to changes.

Embrace Diversity: Be open to different ideas and perspectives. Embrace diversity in all forms, including cultural, gender, age, and race. By doing so, you can learn from people with different experiences and backgrounds and broaden your understanding of the world.

Be Curious: Too many of us lose our curiosity after high school and college. Don't do it. Cultivate a curiosity about the world around you. Ask questions, challenge assumptions, and seek new experiences. Your curiosity will develop a sense of wonder and a desire to learn more about the world.

Drilling Down on Curiosity

Here are some ways to cultivate a curious mindset and inspire yourself to become a continuous learner:

Seek New Experiences: Break out of your comfort zone and try something new. Whether it's trying a new type of food or taking up a new hobby, stepping into the unknown inspires curiosity and opens your mind to new possibilities.

Ask Questions: Be curious about the world around you and don't be afraid to ask questions. The answers will help you gain new insights and perspectives that you may not otherwise have considered.

Read and Watch Informative Content: Reading books and articles and watching documentaries on topics both new and familiar will help you learn more about the world and inspire new areas of interest.

Connect with Others: Engage with those who have different perspectives and experiences than you do. Listening to their stories and insights can help you broaden your understanding of the world and inspire a curious mindset.

Embrace Failure: Failure is an opportunity to learn and grow. By taking risks and trying new things, you'll inevitably make mistakes, but those mistakes will lead to valuable lessons and insights.

Stay Open-Minded: Avoid being too rigid in your beliefs and opinions. Instead, stay open-minded and consider new ideas and perspectives. This will help you stay curious and engaged in the learning process.

Let's face facts: Becoming a generalist is a lot of fun work. It's not studying in one silo until you've perfected the topic. Instead, it's studying simultaneously in multiple silos to broaden the reach of your experiential knowledge.

Learning is a continuous process and it's never too late to develop new skills or improve existing ones. Whether you're a student, a professional, or someone who simply enjoys learning new things, there are specific techniques and strategies that can help you become a better learner. I will explore powerful learning methods later in this book, so you'll have a solid foundation for developing a personal learning plan in any discipline that captures your interest, a plan designed by you that that works for you. For now, absorb the mindset that will expand your thinking.

Fishing for Expertise

In my legal career I was a trial lawyer, the kind you see schmoozing juries and cross-examining witnesses on TV. I spent my life in a courtroom litigating matters that required me to be an "instant expert" in topics like arson investigation (see the prologue). We'll discuss this in more detail in a later chapter, but let's look here at how it works.

First, there was nothing special about this; it came with the job. I needed to be the expert at whatever the case entailed. And sometimes—a *lot* of the time—it entailed things about which I knew less than nothing.

But I had to be an instant expert. The alternative could be a seriously bad day for my client. How did I do it? How did I quickly master topics, and master them so well that I could go toe-to-toe with people who had devoted their lives to learning about the very same things that I needed to master in months? How did I pull it off?

Let's begin at the bottom. What is an expert? An expert is a person with a comprehensive and authoritative knowledge of, or a skill in, a particular area.

When an expert appears in a courtroom, it's the lawyer's job—my job—to question and test the expert's opinion. That means that I must know as much about the topic as the person

I am interrogating to survive the battle of wits unscathed. An in-court expert cannot testify unless the court is satisfied that the individual has comprehensive and authoritative knowledge in the area in which the person is called to testify. Lawyers get to challenge their qualifications to prevent this from happening. *Hey, expert! If I can prove you aren't good enough, you're out.* The more I delved into an expert's background, the more important it was that I be at my best.

I have battled with experts on DNA, entomology, and fire investigation, among various other sciences. I also had the opportunity to question an expert in the flora and fauna of Pennsylvania's Susquehanna Valley. What kind of person is an expert in such a narrow field as that? In this case, it was a fisherman.

I was knee-deep in a major murder case, and I had to establish the exact time a "body in a box" was rolled down a hill. The photos of the scene showed that, looking up the hill from the box in question, all the foliage was knocked over and flattened. I needed to establish the time that this had occurred. It seemed to me that if a box had rolled over the plant life, the plants would have been knocked over. So far so good. Later that morning, when I visited the scene, I saw that the plant life was upright.

A fisherman was working the waters by the riverside, so I clambered down the hill in my expensive courtroom shoes to pay him a visit. As we chatted about his unsuccessful morning, I noticed that my path down the hill was clearly marked by footsteps of flattened vegetation.

After listening to thirty minutes of stories about smallmouth bass, catfish, and bears I looked back up the hill: The once-flattened plants were upright and full once again. I wondered aloud at how quickly the trampled plants restored themselves to lushness. The fisherman's reply? "That doesn't take long once the sun comes up."

What? Hold that thought! Rewind. "So if the plants are flat, what does that mean?"

He replied, "Look where you came down. It all went right back up 'cause the sun is out, but in the morning the plants wait for the sun."

Everything was coming into focus now. "How long have you been fishing here?"

"Twenty years."

Bingo! I took his phone number and, based on his years of experience at the river, his observations, and his opinion, I was able to qualify him as an expert in the narrow focus of the flora and fauna of Pennsylvania's Susquehanna Valley to establish that the body had been dumped earlier than twenty minutes past sunrise.

That fisherman was an expert. His years of knowledge along the banks of the river withstood the challenges of the defense counsel's interrogation. He knew his stuff and he proved it. From that experience, I realized that expertise comes in different shapes and sizes. This little old man was an expert in a small, narrow scope of knowledge that was beyond the realm of what common people know.

Choose Wisely

What do you want to be an expert in? That is the controlling question and one that must be considered before you embark on your journey toward expertise.

If you want to be an expert in woodworking, consider:
- Do you want to be an expert in carpentry?
- Do you want to be an expert in framing a house?
- Do you want to build cabinets?
- Do you want to be an expert in replacing the trim around your kitchen door?
- Do you want to repair your dining room table?

Your answer will set in motion the timetable for your journey.

In his 2008 book *Outliers: The Story of Success,* Malcom Gladwell coined the phrase the *10,000-hour rule.* He suggested that the key to becoming an expert is to devote at least 10,000 hours to the study and practice of a subject. (His assertion is based on a 1993 study in which researchers found that the most accomplished violinists at a specific music academy spent an average of 10,000 hours practicing their instrument).

The 10,000-hour rule may be true for many skills, but not necessary for all. I would also point out that 10,000 hours was the average. Some students became experts in far less time.

Let's also distinguish that *skill* and *knowledge* are distinctly different things. We all know that old saying that "Those who can, do; those who can't, teach." Sadly, that adage diminishes the expertise of many teachers. Many of my professors, in both engineering and law, were respected, world-class experts, but they still didn't "do."

So let's look back at the list of woodworking expertise questions. You might be able to do an expert installation of door trim after receiving a three-hour hands-on tutorial by a contractor, but framing a house could take several months of on-site work with an experienced framer. What journey you choose is based on the breadth and depth of the expertise that you decide to pursue. Choose wisely.

Lumbering toward Expertise

When I was in my late teens I worked as a delivery boy in a lumberyard, but I wanted to be a cabinetmaker. Focused. Narrow. But highly technical. I was already trained as carpenter from a young age (My dad was a master carpenter) so I wasn't starting from square one. I went to my boss, Junior, and promised him I would stick around for two years if I could move from delivery to fabrication. He agreed and I got to work alongside Bob.

Bob was an artist with wood. For two years I worked as his protégé on weekends and after school. I learned from a master. How did this come about?

First, I got the two-year time frame from Bob. I had asked him how long it would take for him to teach me to build flawless cabinetry. He said, "I dunno, maybe a year?" I figured that was a year of full-time work, so I said, "Can you do it in two years part time?"

Bob replied, "Yep. Get me a beer and make sure Junior signs off."

I started with Bob. He was my chosen mentor.

Always Look for a Mentor

Sure, you can use TikTok and YouTube, but nothing beats experience. Bob was able to give me solid advice that resulted in me building an amazing set of oak bookshelves and library showpieces and—unlike Bob—not lose any fingers to the table saw along the way. The artistry of fine cabinetry was a narrow area of expertise that later in life gave me the basic training I needed to build and design all the finished woodwork in my home.

How to find a mentor of your own? Specifically define your desired area of expertise, then find someone who does what you want to do. Can you meet them? If not, have they written works you can study? Some of my mentors haven't been physically present in my life, but they've been mentally present by written word.

Once you've determined your scope of desired expertise, and you've found a go-to source, figure out how much time you're willing or able to commit. Compare that with the amount of time you'll need to reach your goal-level of expertise. How do you do that? Ask your mentor! Or, if your mentor lives only on the printed page, determine it by analysis. A few minutes with Google should give you an idea of what's required.

You're not going to make the journey from Xbox golfer to PGA golfer in only twenty hours. For that, you'll probably need to look back at Gladwell's 10,000-hour rule. If, on the other hand, you want to be an expert putter to impress your golf buddies, then a mentor, a course of study, and visits to the putting green may take far less time than the Gladwell rule.

Your Why, Your Passion

Next, get in touch with the purpose behind your quest and make sure it fills you with the passion you'll need to keep you going through the process of gaining expertise. In my case, it was an emotional goal. I wanted to work with wood like my father did. For others, it's a career goal. Do you need a thorough knowledge of ocean-water salinity to get ahead in your job? Time to get cracking! Or maybe it's a spiritual goal. If you're a recent convert to a new faith you'll have a lifetime of learning to catch up on. Make sure your purpose fills you with the passion you'll need to reach your goal.

Flies: More than You Want to Know

Here's rather unusual example of how I worked with a mentor and followed a course of study to achieve a defined scope of expertise.

Roll back the hands of time to that same murder trial where I had to figure out how long it took flattened vegetation to spring back to life. The defense was disputing the time of death. They had hired an expert named Neal Haskell from Jasper County, South Carolina who buried dead pigs and monitored the birth, growth, and life of larvae that fed on their carcasses. He was going to use bugs to determine the time of death, and he called this witchcraft *forensic entomology*. This was 1992. Who ever heard of forensic entomology in 1992? And what do dead pigs have to do with human remains? Even better: This guy's South Carolina license plate was MAGGOT. Seriously? This had to be a joke, pseudoscience at best. Or was it?

Regardless of my feelings and opinions, one thing was clear: I alone had to cross examine this expert in court.

I started calling people. Remember, this was 1992. There was no internet, and CSI and the litany of Dick Wolf crime dramas were far in the future. I was getting nowhere. I contacted the Ag Sciences Department at Penn State. They had a guy who worked with bugs. He knew nothing about forensics, but he was a bug guy. I had to meet him! But first, I had him send me whatever he could on larvae, black fly larvae to be specific. I waited for the mail to arrive.

Then I called any prosecutor I could find who might have known the guy from South Carolina who, it turned out, kept his forensic lab in his mother's basement. Not a lot to go on.

After days of calling around I learned several things. One, Neal Haskell WAS forensic entomology. Two, he had successfully testified multiple times. Third, he had no worthy adversaries. Dang. That meant I was on my own. I had to cross examine the only expert in his field and I had thirty days to prepare the rest of the case—including a brand-new thing called DNA testing—and I had to go toe-to-toe with an expert with no peers. (I also spent several days holed up in a dive motel being educated by Dr Robin Cotton years before her fame in the O.J. Simpson Case, but let's leave that tale for another day.)

What did I have? A box of black fly larvae research, several facsimiles of testimony and commentary from people who had lost to Haskell, and a scientist at Penn State. The Penn State research was the closest I had to firsthand data, and the faxes from prosecutors were my third-party views of my target. I needed to become an expert in this unknown science of forensic entomology, and I needed to be an expert on Neal Haskell.

I read and studied the two sets of information I had. I digested everything I could about the eggs, larvae, and growth patterns of the black fly. I had no information about how they grew and matured on a human corpse. I did read that the pig corpses were rather like human corpses, but the actual research was limited to the writings of Dr. Haskell.

With bottles of preserved larvae from evidence in tow, I went to Penn State to meet Haskell's closest competitor, Dr. Tang. He welcomed me to his lab, and I spent a full day looking at actual physical specimens. The research came to life. I saw Tang's experiments firsthand and immersed myself in his work. He agreed to be my mentor and to spend the next three weeks teaching me what I needed to know about black flies, their eggs, their birth, and the growth of their larvae on a cadaver as presented by Haskell. My scope of expertise was narrow.

Finally, the trial arrived. Haskell testified. I was his only adversary and I examined him as a peer. I stood my ground, asked the necessary questions, and tested his mettle. I did my job. For that one trial I, too, was a forensic entomologist. I knew the science, the practicum, and the application. Sadly, Haskell's research was flawless. Nonetheless, my pride was intact when the judge approached me at the end of the day to compliment my expertise on the emerging science of forensic entomology.

About ten years later, my wife, also a prosecutor at the time, asked me to recommend a forensic entomologist. I told her to contact Haskell. I had continued to follow his work and knew he had moved from pigs to human cadavers. Impressive.

As Deb and Haskell worked together, he saw her last name and shared that, earlier in his career, he had confronted another Curcillo in a courtroom and all he remembered was that, as he testified, "He grilled me and kept rolling his eyes like I was an idiot."

She replied, "Yep, that's my husband. That's what he does when he knows he has nothing to argue." She was right. That was what I wanted the jury to see as I danced during cross examination. Score.

But that's getting off track. The result was that I had more than held my own in an emerging scientific field that had exactly one expert. I did it by defining my desired area of expertise and boxing it in until it couldn't escape. You can do it, too. The more you learn, the more you may choose to narrow or broaden the purpose behind your objectives. I have used the above approach in the areas of DNA evidence, arson investigations, radiology, toxicology, and other areas that, until I applied myself, I knew little to nothing about.

Let me reiterate: Purpose, commitment, and passion, are the components of the process that will drive all you do. I am known to joke about being "the world's worst guitarist." There's a reason. I know the fret board. I understand the Pythagorean theory behind the notes and frets. But I have never found a purpose other than simple enjoyment to inspire me to commit to translating my knowledge into the skill of a master. Maybe someday, but not today. I don't have the purpose, commitment, and passion. I still derive great joy from the instrument as a hack. It's a choice.

JOURNEY MILEPOSTS

- **The Path to Success and Happiness:** We discussed four key steps to achieving success and happiness: identifying your interests and strengths, setting goals and priorities, managing your time and resources, and cultivating resilience and a growth mindset. How will these steps resonate with your life goals?

- **Multidisciplinary Knowledge:** We have shared the importance of cultivating multidisciplinary knowledge and skills. How does being a generalist benefit your personal and professional growth? Have you actively pursued diverse areas of interest to become more multidisciplinary?

- **Continuous Learning and Curiosity:** Great weight and significance is placed on lifelong learning and curiosity. Reflect on your own attitude toward learning. Do you actively seek new experiences, ask questions, and stay open to new ideas and perspectives?

- **Expertise and Mentoring:** You read about my experiences of needing to become an instant expert in various fields. How important do you think having a mentor is when trying to gain expertise in a specific area? Have you ever sought a mentor? How did it impact your learning journey?

- **Choose Your Area of Expertise:** Before you choose to become an expert consider the exact focus of the area in which you wish to gain expertise. It will make it more manageable, and you will be much more likely to achieve your goal. Have you considered what you want to be an expert in? How did you arrive at that decision?

- **Passion and Purpose:** Purpose, commitment, and passion are the keys that will drive you forward. Reflect on your own experiences. Have you ever pursued a goal or skill without a deep sense of purpose or passion? How did it affect your journey? How great was the feeling of accomplishment?

5

Lane Hoppers: Innovators, Integrators, and Disruptors

For the past 33 years, I have looked in the mirror every morning and asked myself: 'If today were the last day of my life, would I want to do what I am about to do today?' And whenever the answer has been no for too many days in a row, I know I need to change something.
— Steve Jobs

In a world that is increasingly complex and interconnected, the multidisciplinary mindset is a valuable and necessary player in solving complex problems. Being a generalist myself, I have always been fascinated by the impact of multidisciplinary geniuses.

In this chapter we'll wander through hundreds of years of people who had a lane but couldn't seem to stay in it. They hopped and jumped with the agility, adaptability, and cunning of a fox; they lane hopped to innovate, entertain, and change the world. I am thrilled to introduce you to some of my favorites!

The Best Thing Since...?

In the bustling world of the early 20th century, a jeweler and optician from Davenport, Iowa would become an unlikely hero of the bread industry. Otto Rohwedder was a successful jeweler, owning and operating three stores in St. Joseph, Missouri. He then branched out and studied optics at the Northern Illinois College of Ophthalmology and Otology. Despite this venture into a new career, in 1916 he sold everything to move back to Davenport and pursue a revolutionary new idea—a bread-slicing machine!

In the early 20th century, American bread was soft and plush and difficult to slice. This is where Otto's machine came in. It allowed people to slice their bread quickly and easily, producing a perfect slice every time. Otto even created a machine that packaged the sliced bread to prolong its freshness.

The nation's bakers revolted. Who on earth would want someone else slicing their bread? But, far from being dead on arrival, Otto's patented invention was a hit. He sold his first machine to the Chillicothe Baking Company and the first loaf of sliced bread was sold on July 7, 1928. When it was picked up by Wonder Bread in 1930, demand for pre-sliced bread skyrocketed, outselling traditional loaves by 1933. The slicer revolutionized the bread industry and made life easier for people all over the world.

Thanks to the innovation of Otto Rohwedder, a jeweler, entrepreneur, optician, and self-taught engineer, American life was changed forever. Sliced bread revolutionized the bread industry by making it easier and more convenient to prepare and eat bread. It increased the shelf life of bread and made it possible to ship pre-sliced loaves across longer distances. It made the double-slice toaster a fixture in American kitchens, it led to the development of a zillion sandwich recipes, it opened up vast new marketing opportunities, and it sparked the growth of packaged foods that, for better and for worse, have conquered our supermarkets.

Walk into your nearest mini market and pause. Every prepackaged item you see resulted from Rohwedder's multidisciplinary journey.

A Screen in Every Home

But the story doesn't end there. Let's turn the channel to another world-changing invention that we take for granted: television. By 1952, TV was on the ascendant and Hollywood was having a fit, much like the baking industry did when Otto introduced the industrial bread slicer. They were all, like, "No way, TV isn't going anywhere! We've got a monopoly on movies, baby!" They saw television as a threat and they didn't want it to succeed. Yes, television was once a disruptive innovation.

When Red Skelton, a hilarious comic and a fixture in homes across America, was asked about the future of TV, he said something profound: "Don't worry about television. *It's the best thing since sliced bread.*"

Well, that was the birth of that idiom. It was a public acknowledgment of Otto Roherdder as a multidisciplinary, reaching into a different lane, and doing something that had never been done before, something so incredible that it changed everything.

To be multidisciplinary is not to challenge the status quo simply because you embrace disruption. To be multidisciplinary is to challenge your own status quo by jumping out of your lane and into a multitude of others. It pays off. As Otto rightly predicted, not many of us have broken bread in the last 24 hours, but we have all touched a slice of bread.

Triple Threat!

In old Hollywood, there were performers who were jacks-of-all-trades: actors/dancers/jugglers/you name it. These people were known as *slashies* (get it?) or *triple threats*. It was their versatility that made them valuable. They could be cast in many roles and adapt more easily to whatever role they were given. Their multiple lanes were seen as assets rather than weaknesses.

I had the privilege of interviewing Todd Fisher, a dear friend who was immersed in the world of old Hollywood. Todd grew up as the son of Debbie Reynolds and the brother of Carrie Fisher, but he had the distinct honor of not being the one on camera. He was the one behind the camera, the producer, the director, and the CEO of the Debbie Reynolds Hotel and Casino. Todd is truly multidisciplinary with a deep understanding of the workings of the entertainment industry. A simple discussion with him makes one take a journey back into the old days of Hollywood.

Back then, the movie production business was a well-oiled machine that churned out hit after hit. But how did they do it? They utilized multidisciplinary individuals. In the early days of Hollywood, filmmakers didn't have the high-tech equipment we have today. They had to rely on their creativity and resourcefulness to get the job done. This meant that many of the people who worked in the movie industry were multidisciplinary. They had to be experts in a variety of fields, from acting and writing to directing and producing.

For example, Orson Welles was an actor, director, producer, writer, and magician, among other things. He brought all of his talents to bear on his films, creating masterpieces like *Citizen Kane* that continue to be celebrated today. And then there was Walt Disney, who was an animator, producer, and entrepreneur. He had a vision for his films and theme parks that was ahead of its time. His multidisciplinary approach helped him create some of the most beloved characters and stories of all time.

The old Hollywood system relied on these people who are good for more than one thing to create products that were both entertaining and profitable. They understood that having people who were experts in multiple fields would give them an edge in a highly competitive industry.

While the movie business has changed dramatically, the concept of utilizing multidisciplinary individuals is still important. In fact, it's becoming more essential in all walks of life as we navigate an increasingly complex and interconnected world.

These multiple-threat people pulled from different disciplines, and did things so differently that they remained in high demand and made some of the greatest films in history. So let's take a page from the old Hollywood playbook and embrace our multidisciplinary talents. Who knows, we might just create something truly amazing!

Beyond the Big Screen

Hedy Lamarr was a Hollywood icon and actress in the 1930s and 1940s, but she was also a talented inventor and engineer. Born in Austria in 1914, Lamarr showed an early interest in technology and was particularly intrigued by the possibilities of radio communication.

During World War II Lamarr began working on a secret project with composer George Antheil to develop a communication system that could not be jammed by enemy forces. Their invention, which they called *frequency hopping,* involved sending radio signals over different frequencies in a pattern that was synchronized between the transmitter and receiver.

Lamarr and Antheil received a patent for their invention in 1942, but the U.S. Navy wasn't interested. It wasn't until the 1960s that frequency hopping technology was adopted for use in military communications and, later, it became the basis for modern technologies such as GPS, Bluetooth, and Wi-Fi.

Despite her groundbreaking work in engineering, Lamarr faced discrimination in Hollywood and was often dismissed as a beautiful but vapid actress. It wasn't until later in life that she received recognition for her contributions to technology and was inducted into the National Inventors Hall of Fame in 2014.

Lamarr's legacy as an inventor and engineer serves as a reminder of the importance of recognizing and supporting women in STEM fields. Her invention of frequency hopping was truly ahead of its time and has had a lasting impact on modern communication technology. She was the ultimate quadruple threat. Her mind lived in a perpetual cross-disciplinary state.

Three Plus One

I believe that professional *quadruple threats* are an asset to many situations, businesses, and opportunities. Whether you call them Jacks and Jills of all trades, multi-hyphen professionals, or people who live wide, they combine multiple careers, talents, and streams of income into a much fuller life and a wider existence.

From sliced bread, and the little screen to the big screen, to the computer monitor—that's where Richard Garriott comes in.

Garriott is an Anglo-American entrepreneur, video game developer, and space traveler, widely known for creating the popular *Ultima* series of computer games in the 1980s and 1990s. He is also a co-founder of Origin Systems, a company that produced several successful immersive video games, including *Ultima Online*.

In addition to his achievements in the video game industry, Garriott has a passion for space exploration. He became the sixth private individual to travel to space in 2008, aboard the Soyuz TMA-13 spacecraft, and spent 12 days aboard the International Space Station.

Garriott was one of the pioneers of online gaming. *Ultima Online,* one of the first massively multiplayer online role-playing games (MMORPGs), released in 1997, was a groundbreaking game that introduced many of the features that are now standard in MMORPGs, such as player housing, player-run economies, and a persistent game world.

In creating this virtual world, Garriott paid extreme attention to details with the goal of creating an experience so immersive that, for the players, the real world would cease to exist. He brought to the table a diverse background culled from a life of exploration, research, and knowledge.

To create the humanistic side of the game, he studied every religious discipline in the world. His insatiable desire to explore gave him an encyclopedic grasp of global cultures. Armed with this knowledge and his explorative nature, he created a universe where players' actions could be judged right and wrong by a sophisticated code of ethics, as opposed to just shooting everyone. Once inside the Ultima universe they discovered an endless landscape meant to be explored much like Earth was in centuries past.

The creation of the MMORPG was the product of a truly multidisciplinary mind with an insatiable appetite for learning and discovering new things. Everything that Garriott did then paved the way for virtual reality today. Consider the fact that Richard Garriott has been to the space station *and* to the Mariana Trench—the deepest part of the ocean—and he put the same profound intensity and experience into his programming. This is the result of someone who is a lifelong learner and is dedicated to discovery. He pulled knowledge from every lane he lived in and brought it into the digital world to change online gaming forever. That is disruption and cross-disciplinary thinking at work.

Let's Fly a Kite

Earlier in this book I spoke of Walt Whitman. The bridge named for him, in Philadelphia, is only a few miles up the Delaware River from another bridge, named after one of history's greatest cross-disciplinary thinkers, Ben Franklin.

Benjamin Franklin, a pivotal figure in American history, epitomized the essence of cross-disciplinary thinking long before the term was coined. At the very core of his varied pursuits was an insatiable curiosity that refused to be tethered to any single discipline. A printer by trade, Franklin's interests meandered through science, politics, writing, and inventing, making him a true polymath.

His journey into science resulted in his legendary kite-and-key experiment. This venture didn't stand isolated; it integrated with his inventive spirit, leading to the creation of the lightning rod. In the realm of literature, Franklin's *Poor Richard's Almanack* masterfully wove humor, wisdom, and social commentary, revealing his knack for understanding the human condition.

Politically, he stood as a diplomat and a key figure in the drafting of the U.S. Constitution, leveraging his diverse knowledge and insights to shape the early foundations of the nation. His communal spirit, paired with his understanding of societal needs, gave birth to America's first public library, volunteer fire department, and even a post-secondary institution, the University of Pennsylvania.

Franklin's life was a tapestry of interconnected disciplines. He never saw the world through a narrow lens but rather perceived the intricate web of relationships between varied fields. In doing so, he not only left an indelible mark on multiple domains but also demonstrated the limitless possibilities that arise when one embraces a cross-disciplinary approach to life and work. His legacy serves as a powerful reminder that breaking barriers between disciplines can lead to innovations that stand the test of time.

Frankly, a reading of his autobiography reveals that Ben Franklin hopped between lanes more in a single day than some do in a lifetime.

A Bite of the Apple

Steve Jobs wasn't just a tech maverick; he exemplified cross-disciplinary thinking at its finest, demonstrating that true innovation lives at the intersection of varied fields. An early testament to this mindset was his decision to drop into a calligraphy course at Reed College. While it seemed unrelated to the trajectory of a future tech giant, this experience profoundly impacted Apple's design philosophy. Jobs integrated the artistry of calligraphy into the realm of computing, introducing elegant typefaces and proportional fonts to the Macintosh, seamlessly blending the worlds of art and technology.

But Jobs's synthesis of disciplines didn't stop at design aesthetics. He consistently drew from a vast array of fields to guide Apple's path to dominance. His passion for music birthed the iPod and iTunes, transforming the music industry by combining tech with an understanding of the arts and consumer desires. And then there was Pixar, his foray into the movies, where he once again merged technology with storytelling, reshaping the animation industry.

Jobs had an uncanny ability to see connections where others saw boundaries. He didn't view technology, design, art, or entertainment as separate entities but as fully integrated lanes of a larger narrative. Jobs changed not only the way we engage with technology but also how we perceive its role in broader cultural and aesthetic contexts. His cross-disciplinary approach is a testament to the power of looking beyond one's immediate field, showing us that the most impactful innovations often come from the melding of diverse perspectives and skills.

Decoding the Human Psyche

Carl Jung, a Swiss psychiatrist and psychoanalyst, was the pioneering mind behind Analytical Psychology. Renowned for his concepts of the collective unconscious and archetypes, Jung's work beautifully bridged the realms of psychology, spirituality, and the arts, offering a holistic understanding of the human psyche.

Jung wasn't just a psychiatrist; he was a voracious learner who didn't believe in strictly defined boundaries when it came to knowledge. While most know him for his pioneering work in psychology, Jung's genius was in how seamlessly he weaved together insights from a variety of fields, setting a gold standard for interdisciplinary thought.

His journey to India is a testament to his boundary-crossing curiosity. While there, he didn't just absorb; he integrated. Delving into Eastern spiritualities and philosophies, he recognized patterns and ideas that resonated with Western psychological concepts. This wasn't just a superficial fusion. Jung's exploration led to his idea of the collective unconscious, a theory suggesting shared symbols and patterns across humanity, irrespective of culture. It's as if he was painting a masterpiece, and India added colors he hadn't known existed.

Alchemy, for many, is ancient history. But Jung, with his cross-disciplinary mindset, saw it differently. Instead of an obsolete pseudoscience, he found in alchemy a rich symbolic system that mirrored his psychological theories. The transformation of base metals into gold? For Jung, this echoed the personal journey of growth and self-awareness.

Art and religion weren't just cultural or spiritual expressions to Jung. They were repositories of human experience and emotion. Artworks from different times and places, he believed, held clues to universal human experiences. They weren't just beautiful or profound; they were doorways into the human psyche. Similarly, religious texts weren't just doctrines but a roadmap to the shared spiritual and emotional landscapes of humanity.

Carl Jung epitomizes what it means to be a cross-disciplinary thinker. In his work, fields like art, alchemy, religion, and mythology weren't separate from psychology; they were integral parts of it. He stands as a beacon, illuminating the rich insights that come from breaking down walls between disciplines, from seeing the world not as fragmented territories of knowledge, but as an interconnected web of wisdom.

A Fall from SpaceX?

Sometimes disruption, and disruptive people, creates controversy. That is certainly true of our next multidiscipinarian.

Elon Musk, a South African-born entrepreneur, is revered for his multidisciplinary background which spans across sectors such as electric vehicles, space travel, and online payments. His journey began with a web software company called Zip2, which was sold in 1999 for $307 million, earning Musk $22 million for his share. Following this venture, Musk initiated another startup, PayPal, which also saw enormous success and further established his reputation in Silicon Valley. His ambitious pursuits didn't end there. Musk founded SpaceX with an aim to make space travel more accessible, and later took over Tesla, making it one of the key players in the electric vehicle market.

Musk's rise to become one of the world's wealthiest individuals was marked by his relentless work ethic and ability to disrupt traditional markets with innovative technology, but his journey hasn't been without controversy. In recent times, especially following his 2022 acquisition of Twitter, Musk has faced criticism for his management decisions and political thoughts. Twitter—now X—saw a significant drop in user numbers and company value, alongside a notable increase in misinformation and hate speech under his ownership.

Musk rose to the top of his game and, love him or hate him, his wealth puts him at the top of most people's games. But unfortunately, the risk taking, continuous drive to keep interested in things, and inability to sit still that multidisciplinarians experience, has—in Musk—resulted in rather outlandish behavior. It's fair to say that his financial freedom has him sitting on a pile of money he cannot possibly lose. That height gives him a lack of interest in what people think of him. Nonetheless, his multilane existence has changed the way we move money and do business online.

The Common Denominator

Everyone we discussed above is what I call a *focused generalist,* someone with a very focused career and specialization, but an external learning experience that allows them to dabble in multidisciplinary environments.

What Happened to Liberal Arts?

As you may have noticed, I have lived the life of a generalist. While most of my career was focused on being an attorney and building a successful law firm, my extracurricular interests are, and have been, diverse. I never turn down an opportunity to learn and it is in this spirit that I say to you that the multidisciplinary approach to life and business is amazing. A diversity of experience, the cross-disciplinary thought process, and the continuous use of both left- and right-brain thinking, provide extraordinary benefits (which we'll get into a little later).

In the 1980s, when I was in college, there was pressure to specialize. In fact, a guidance counselor who pushed someone toward liberal arts was usually implying that the student couldn't make it in anything else. How wrong they were.

I told my high school guidance counselor that I wanted to earn an engineering degree and then go to law school. I was told that made no sense. I was also told that I would never get into law school with an engineering degree. My guidance counselor shrugged off my desire, commenting that while I did well in class, I didn't know how life worked. Besides, he said, "You probably should go to art school since you're the guy that paints all the stage sets. That is something you would be good at."

Yes, I know guidance counselors are dream killers, but I always wondered if I should hunt down my guidance counselor and tell him how wrong he was, but it's probably too late for that.

When I was in school, and worked toward my engineering degree, I also took as many philosophy classes as I could. My biggest fear at the time was losing my creativity, my innovation, and my artistic ability.

I don't know if I truly understood at the time how beneficial a diverse education would be, but I did know one thing: If I did only one thing I would be bored. I knew that I had to keep both my left and right brain alive and kicking. Experience and knowledge were essential to making me happy.

My experience is not singular. Unfortunately, over the past few decades, the liberal arts degree, which traditionally includes subjects like history, philosophy, literature, and the arts, and has been a staple of higher education for centuries, has experienced a significant decline in popularity. One reason is the increasing academic focus on the job prospects and earning potential associated with various degrees. Students (and parents) seek degrees that will lead to high-paying, stable careers, and the liberal arts are often seen as lacking in practical applications, leading to a decrease in enrollment in liberal arts programs and an increase in enrollment in STEM (science, technology, engineering, and mathematics) programs and vocational education. The idea is that these degrees will provide a clear path to a successful career, while a liberal arts degree may not.

Furthermore, the liberal arts have been criticized for being out of touch with the modern world, that they're primarily focused on historical and cultural topics and not enough on practical, real-world issues. As a result, some students and parents see the liberal arts as irrelevant to the needs of a rapidly changing, technology-driven world.

Despite these criticisms, many educators and employers still value the liberal arts degree. They argue that the liberal arts provide students with valuable critical thinking, communication, and problem-solving skills, necessary for success in any career. Additionally, the liberal arts can help students develop a broader worldview and a deeper understanding of the human experience, which is important in our diverse and interconnected global society.

On a positive note, my references to the demise of the liberal arts degree may be overstated, as some universities are adapting to changing times by offering interdisciplinary programs that combine the liberal arts with more practical subjects. For example, some universities are offering degrees in digital humanities, which combine traditional liberal arts subjects with digital technologies. See what they did there? They gave a liberal arts degree a moniker that sounds a lot like specialization.

Most of All, It's a Blast

The bottom line, however, among all of these people in history and talk of changing educational trends, is this: A multidisciplinary life is a fun life. You will feel balanced because you will be in control of what you learn. You will be in control of what you do.

I can assure you that when I was in school, I wished it would all stop. I felt like I was being bounced around and controlled by my teachers. But then, as I started to find my own way of mastering disciplines and learning, I hand-selected the people I would work with and study from. It was all my own doing, and it was all my choice. That's the difference. In *choosing* the multidisciplinary life you choose to be a lifelong student of the world.

In high school, I was all about learning art, and I was even accepted into the prestigious Moore College of Art and Design in Philadelphia. Then I made the crazy decision to turn down that opportunity and pursue a degree in civil engineering from Temple University. Then I went to law school. Throughout law school I worked as a cabinetmaker. I still do all the woodwork in my house.

During the COVID-19 pandemic I picked up a paintbrush and went back to canvas painting. I am honored to have my art hanging in some very prestigious locations—I never anticipated that, but it sure feels good. Throughout my law career I have also been an entertainer for children's parties, and now I'm a magician and a mentalist (a "mind reader") at corporate events. My wife and I even had a mail-order business at one point supplying props to magicians around the world.

Every time I see an Amazon commercial where their people talk about how the company helps them get higher educations and become multidisciplinary, I get even more excited about the world we live in. When I was young we were driven to be specialists. I had to fight for every opportunity to learn something new. Even when I wanted to learn philosophy, the engineering school told me no. They had rules against dual majors. But the world is changing, and we are once again discovering the power of the multidisciplinary generalist.

Be Multitudes!

By broadening your knowledge and skills you can unlock new ways of thinking, problem-solving, and creating. You'll learn to connect the dots in ways that others cannot, and you'll become more well-rounded and adaptable.

Becoming multidisciplinary is not an easy path, but it is a rewarding one. It requires courage to step outside your comfort zone and embrace the unknown. But the benefits are immeasurable. You will become more creative, more resilient, and more valuable to your organization and society as a whole. Let's embrace our contradictions and complexities. Let's celebrate the many different parts of ourselves, recognizing that they all contribute to making us who we are, and let's extend that same celebration to those around us, recognizing that they, too, are vast and contain multitudes.

I challenge you to take the first step toward becoming multidisciplinary. Whether it's taking a class in a new subject, attending a conference outside your field, or simply talking to someone with a different perspective, start exploring the vast possibilities that lie beyond your current expertise. It's a transformative journey waiting to unfold.

You're on the cusp of a remarkable transformation, and you won't regret the incredible journey that awaits. Anyone with an insatiable appetite to try new things and discover new lines of operation possesses the ability to change the world.

What other disciplines can you explore today? Who knows what could transform our world next?

JOURNEY MILEPOSTS

- **The Impact of Multidisciplinary Geniuses:** Consider the profound impact that multidisciplinary geniuses can have when they venture into new lanes. How have individuals who crossed disciplinary boundaries influenced our world, and what can we learn from their journeys?

- **Innovations That Change the World:** Reflect on the idea that individuals who have experience in multiple disciplines often create inventions and innovations that reshape industries. How does the story of sliced bread serve as a metaphor for transformative change? What other innovations can you think of that had a similar impact?

- **The Lifelong Learner's Path:** Explore the concept of multidisciplinary geniuses as lifelong learners dedicated to discovery. What role does insatiable curiosity and the willingness to explore new realms play in their success? How can you apply this mindset in your own life?

- **Driving Innovation Across Fields:** Think about how multidisciplinary thinking can drive innovation in seemingly unrelated fields. Are there examples from your own experiences where diverse knowledge or skills have led to creative solutions or breakthroughs?

- **Empowering Individuals for Change:** Reflect on the idea that anyone with a thirst for trying new things and discovering new opportunities has the potential to make significant changes in the world. How can you embrace this mindset of exploration and adaptability to drive positive change in your life?

- **Bridging Silos for Efficiency:** Consider the role of multidisciplinary individuals as bridges between silos and how they can ensure efficient project execution. How can you leverage your diverse skills and knowledge to facilitate collaboration and effectiveness in your professional endeavors?

BE MORE

6

Be a Fox: Versatile, Adaptable, and Agile

*The fox knows many things,
but the hedgehog knows one big thing.*
— Archilochus

As I formulated the outline for this book, I was approached by a visibly stressed law school graduate who wanted to chat about the things I had accomplished, clearly fascinated that a lawyer had lived such a diverse life. After a few minutes, the source of her stress became apparent: She was waiting for the results of the bar exam.

I made an off-the-cuff comment that, increasingly, many people have to take the bar exam more than once before they pass. She asked me how many times I took it and, of course, I told her the truth: once. Apparently, that wasn't the answer she wanted to hear.

I tried to reassure her, but she wouldn't have any of it. The more I wrestled with her emotional instability, the more fixated she became on the pass/fail mindset. So I went out on a limb and asked, "You have a tiger mom, don't you?"

After a pause, she said, "Yes."

She recognized that she was the child of a tiger parent. You know, the helicopter parent who is overly and highly invested in their child's success, the ones who drive them to attain ever-higher levels of achievement, pushing a mindset of focus in one area where failure is never an option. Her mother had prepared her to be a lawyer. There were no other options, no other paths to success. Passing was the only way this young lady would escape the claws of Mom. Any other result would be failure.

I felt bad. She had just heard my keynote, and was captivated by my diverse life. She fixated on the fact that, even through law school, my life had been filled with variety. Her mom had made her give up everything and focus only on her studies and now she began to see what she had sacrificed.

My advice to her? "Whether you pass or fail, the moment you get the result you need to begin to live your life."

That was the first moment in the conversation that I saw her relax. It was only for a moment. Within seconds her mental vision of her mother resurfaced, and she saw nothing but pass or fail. She saw nothing other than the required success that her mother had prepared her for.

The Fox and the Hedgehog

As I walked away, I remembered Aesop's fable of *The Fox and The Hedgehog*. The fable has many iterations, and the version you know may be different from mine, but in the one I recall the fox swims across a rapid river and is exhausted when he reaches the other side. He is immediately attacked by a swarm of flies that feast on his blood. Prone and weak, he was approached by a hedgehog who asked, "Would you like me to help drive the flies from your skin?"

The fox replied, "No."

Confused, the hedgehog asked, "Would it not be less painful if I removed the flies from your skin, my friend?"

"No, I do not want them disturbed," the fox answered. "They have taken hold and drank all the blood they can drink. If you drive them away another greedy swarm will move in and take away what little I have left."

Historically, the moral of this story was that it was better to bear a lesser evil than to risk a greater one but, in tandem with the Greek poet Archilochus's observation that "The fox knows many things, but the hedgehog knows one big thing," this fable is a source of curiosity for me.

In folklore and fairy tales, foxes are characterized as open-minded thinkers who are always learning and know a lot about a bunch of different stuff. They're great at adapting to new situations and can improvise on the fly. On the other hand, hedgehogs are all about one big theory or idea, and they're not really into trying new things. They're stuck in their ways and can be kind of formulaic.

The hedgehog is the specialist and the fox is the generalist. The hedgehog is the metaphorical expert at one thing, a specialist in one area, one with a narrow point of view and scope of knowledge. Their concept of the world is limited by their area of expertise. They tend to stay in their lane. They know one big thing.

The fox, on the other hand, is notoriously sly, keeping options open and seeing actual events in real time. The fox is the metaphorical generalist, skeptical of any view that is restricted to a single lane of knowledge. They see the whole picture and bring a wide array of information into their actions. Being a fox means you can apply knowledge from different fields to solve problems.

Aesop's fable and its poetic reference were further explored and expanded by Isaiah Berlin in his 1953 essay, *The Hedgehog and the Fox: An Essay on Tolstoy's View of History*[1]. Berlin expanded the metaphor to apply the story—and its moral—to divide writers and thinkers into one or the other.

Berlin saw hedgehogs as the ones who viewed the world through the lens of a single defining idea. He saw the ideal hedgehog as one who related to a central vision in a way that all they said had significance. The foxes drew upon a wide variety of experiences with reticence to boil the world down to a single lane. The ideal fox pursues many ends. Often these ends are unrelated and even contradictory. The fox doesn't look at information with an eye towards fitting it into or excluding it from one single embracing vision. The fox performs a balancing act of ideas, concepts, and knowledge.

Further analysis of the fabled duo was provided by Phillip E. Tetlock, Annenberg University professor at the Wharton School and the School of Arts and Sciences, in his seminal 2017

---

[1] Berlin, Isaiah. The Hedgehog and the Fox, Princeton University Press, 2013

book *Expert Political Judgment: How Good is it? How can We Know?*[2] in which he applies Berlin's metaphorical fox and hedgehog to the thinking styles of political advisors. Tetlock takes the position that the fox—the open thinker who knows many things—draws from his eclectic experience and is much better at improvising in response to changing events, and thus is a better predictor. On the contrary, the hedgehog, who knows one big theory, is mired in tradition, formulaic approaches, and poorly defined problems.

In the research that led to *Expert Political Judgment*, Tetlock asked 284 political experts, mostly with postgraduate training as academics, journalists, intelligence analysts, and think-tank members, most with about 12 years of experience in their fields, to assign probabilities to future events. Each of the experts weighed in on approximately 100 situations, totaling about 28,000 forecasts. Great pain was taken to make sure that the questions covered a gamut of topics from economic indicators, national GDPs, and defense leadership changes. Tetlock then looked for consistencies in the opinions. His tongue-in-cheek conclusion? "Partisans across the opinion spectrum are vulnerable to occasional bouts of ideologically induced insanity."

Professor Tetlock was pointing out the powerfully adverse effects of cognitive bias in the decision-making and analytical process. In a later chapter, we will dive into these biases and the filters we use in making decisions, but for now let's look deeper into Professor Tetlock's results.

---

[2] Tetlock, Phillip E. Expert Political Judgment: How Good is it? How can We Know? Princeton University Press, 2017

Digging Into the Results

The results showed that the foxes were more accurate than the hedgehogs in an overall way that could not be reconciled through statistical analysis. Tetlock even tweaked the data in several different ways to see if there were some chance ways to explain the differential. No explanation was found.

Looking at Berlin's analysis and Archilochus's suggestion that the fox knows many things but the hedgehog knows one big thing, Tetlock looked at professors as thinkers who relate everything to a single central vision and make conclusions and observations that are consistent with that vision. For instance, it didn't matter whether someone was a libertarian hedgehog or a Marxist hedgehog. They could've been a conservative hedgehog or a liberal hedgehog. They might have been pessimistic hedgehogs or optimistic hedgehogs. All these classifications were considered in Tetlock's statistical analysis. When all data was considered, the results revealed that the hedgehog approached history and current events in a deductive framework and was less likely to absorb many different facts into the context of their principles.

The foxes, on the other hand, were skeptical of big theories and big ideas. They were not single-topic specialists. While the hedgehogs might have been predisposed to an ideal-driven mindset, the foxes were more open minded; they were more holistic.

The foxes who did the best forecasting were those who were the least enthusiastic about the study. They also weren't enthusiastic about one structure of belief, or favorite theories of political or cultural civilization. The hedgehogs were more enthusiastic about the assignments when they could extend their favorite theories into the data. The specialist mind of the hedgehogs made them more confident going into the study then were the foxes who were more hesitant about their ability to make predictions.

In the end, foxes were better at both short-term and long-term predictions. While the hedgehogs did very well at assigning higher probabilities to big changes that eventually did materialize, the statistics showed that there was a steep cost in false positives. Basically, this means that the specialists/hedgehogs may have known where they were going but, in the end, they were wrong more often than not.

But here's the thing: The hedgehogs weren't totally useless. While they did predict some major events that no one else saw coming, like the collapse of the USSR and the Yugoslavian Civil War, they also made some pretty outlandish predictions, like the collapse of Canada and India.

It also should be noted that the hedgehogs did better collectively than they did separately. This leads me to question whether specialists who can work well together can achieve more, but it also reinforces the ideal interdependency of specialists and generalists.

So what does all of this mean for us? It means that we need both foxes and hedgehogs in our lives and our businesses. They're interdependent. The foxes bring adaptability and creativity, while the hedgehogs bring deep knowledge and focus. When they work together, they can achieve some seriously cool things.

Think about this in your company or your personal life and consider that the hedgehog and the fox are an interdependent ecosystem. The employment of foxes and hedgehogs can have a significant long-term benefit.

Foxes and Hedgehogs in the Real World

Many people want to hire a specialist, someone who's focused on a specific area. If it's an accountant we want an expert accountant; if it's a lawyer we want the best lawyer; if it's a programmer we want the best programmer, and so on. When we do this, we amass a great number of hedgehogs moving in one direction within the funnels of their expertise.

Hedgehogs push big ideas and big dreams as far as they reasonably can. They also push them far *beyond* what's reasonable. Yes, this could be a great benefit to your long-term goals, but consider the fox. Foxes avail themselves of the same raw materials as the hedgehogs, but then they create what Tetlock called a "creative eclectic mishmash" of knowledge that, on average, has more predictive power than the original idea initiated by the hedgehog.

Considering all the above we also know that hedgehogs are more certain about the results. They attach a higher probability of likelihood on their efforts than would the fox. Tetlock's study showed that hedgehogs are two to three times more likely to attach a probability approaching certainty to their conclusions. The fox, being a generalist, is more open to ideas and less certain of results, and is thus more willing to consider possibilities without digging in. Among Tetlock's conclusions, he stated that when hedgehogs "say things are inevitable those things have happened only about 78% of the time and when they say things are impossible those things happen about 20% [of the time].[3]"

Think about the number of times you've heard a specialist say something is certain. The degree of certainty they attach to their statements has a very powerful effect on the listeners. Even in our own lives, if we hear that something is impossible there's a subconscious block to overcoming that possibility. When you or your team are working to become more innovative and creative, *no* has a bad effect. The more we hear something is impossible the more our efforts are stymied.

I don't know about you, but I know I've had many difficult conversations when I had to tell an expert they were wrong. Think about what we see on television and on the news. Experts don't back down. The more immersed someone is in their area of expertise, the more of a specialist they've become, the more certain they are of their own conclusions and thoughts.

Generalists, on the other hand, are more likely to drone on with conditions, disclaimers, and qualifiers, but they are probably more often right than not. The charismatic talking head, who is certain of their statements, and tells a great story

---

[3] Long Now Foundation. Why Foxes Are Better Forecasters Than Hedgehogs | Philip Tetlock. YouTube, 13 April 20, https://www.youtube.com/watch?v=EeHyVauX458

without qualifications and disclaimers, might just be wrong. Frankly, a generalist is more likely to explain their opinion and conclusions because they have a better grasp on why they believe what they believe. They have not gotten lost in the "specialist zone," the zone where everything is so obvious to the expert that they feel no need to explain it.

Generalists in The Workplace

Let's look at the initial benefit of allowing generalists to rise and enter your organization.

Out of the box, they are more willing to be skeptical and challenge your experts in their conclusions. When the expert knows they'll be scrutinized from the get-go, they will look harder and, in my experience, become slightly more foxlike in their endeavor. Consider hiring a generalist to challenge your experts in their conclusions and bring in more knowledge of the world without fixated predispositions. Generalists are more willing to learn from their mistakes and see the big picture. They're more apt to *admit* to making mistakes because they're eager to learn from them. Many generalists love being wrong as much as they love being right.

As we look at the future of the workplace consider that, in January 2021, McKinsey & Company reported that most companies are aware that there is a skill gap among their employees. According to the McKinsey survey, executives say that reskilling is the best way to close a capability gap. Building skills—for example, reskilling existing employees—was ranked at 53% effectiveness.[4] Thus, as we move into the future, people will need to be retrained in their jobs to keep industry moving forward.

The lifelong learner, who is already skilled at learning in multiple lanes and multiple disciplines, is much easier to train. They are in a prime position to learn because it is what they do. Skill development and fungibility is the new mantra.

Looking again at the Tetlock study, we know that a generalist is more open-minded. By becoming multidisciplinary, and cross training your skills, you also become more adaptable. Versatility is a major factor moving forward.

Broadening the Field of Vision

In 1960, Theodore Levitt wrote an article in the *Harvard Business Review* titled "Marketing Myopia"[5]. This article has stood the test of time: When it was re-published in 2004, the *Harvard Business Review* called it "the quintessential big hit HBR piece"[6]. It's also worth noting that the *Harvard Business Review* has republished it at least three times. It does not go away.

This article has stood the test of time because it popularized the idea that companies need to think of themselves as being in the people business, not as producing goods and services, but continually maintaining focus on the customer.

---

[4] McKinsey Quarterly. The Skillful Corporation, https://www.mckinsey.com/capabilities/people-and-organizational-performance/our-insights/five-fifty-the-skillful-corporation 2021
[5] Levitt, Theodore. (1960) Marketing Myopia. Harvard Business Review
[6] Levitt, T. (2004). Marketing Myopia. Best of HBR. Harvard Business Review

Levitt put the spotlight on the railroads. By the mid-20th century, the once massively profitable railroads had become a struggling industry. The railroad moguls, according to Levitt, had failed to understand that they were in the business of *transportation* rather than simply *railroads*. Had they considered this they might not have been overshadowed and overpowered by the automotive, truck, and airplane industries.

Levitt declared that the failure was at the top because the leaders did not anticipate the need to broaden the focus of their companies.

Levitt also called into question Hollywood. He indicated that it was by a slim margin that the motion-picture industry didn't lose everything to television, and it was only kicking and screaming that producers and Hollywood powerhouses were dragged into TV.

As I see it, the so-called experts in both the railroad and motion-picture industries would have benefited from the addition of more generalists among their ranks. When Leavitt wrote his article he took note of the fact that, in the electronics industry, the upper management was top-heavy with engineers and scientists. In his words, this created "a selective bias in favor of research and production at the expense of marketing."[7]

There is a great effort to drag specialists into every business. Leaders believe that specialists can be the end-all and be-all of their success. Unfortunately, the experts and specialists are so narrowly focused on their fields that they lose sight of the big picture.

---

[7] Levitt, Id at p.10.

Tony Fadell is an American engineer, designer, entrepreneur, and investor, the founder and former CEO of Nest. He is also considered to be "the father of the iPod" and the cocreator of the iPhone. Like most successful people, his journey was not easy. Fadell began his career with General Magic, focusing on personal handheld devices. It was there that he created the Sony Magic Link which combined a phone, a touchscreen, apps, games, and email functionality. It was revolutionary. Unfortunately, it was 1994 and the world wasn't ready. The solution he provided wasn't one that people wanted. I know that today that sounds completely absurd, but it was a 1994 reality. In his 2022 book *Build: An Unorthodox Guide to Making Things Worth Making,* Fadell stated that, as General Magic was falling apart, he knew he had to shift his focus. "General magic was making incredible technology but wasn't making a product that would solve real people's problems. But I thought it could."[8] He went on to say, "'If you make it, they will come' doesn't always work. If the technology isn't ready they won't come for sure. But even if you've got the tech, then you still have to time it right. The world has to be ready to watch it."[9]

Fadell is clearly a specialist, and he greatly understands the technology and the software. His vision is second to none, but I also picture he and his partners celebrating the invention of the Magic Link, partying in the office and playing games on it, excited by what they had created. They wouldn't have been cooped up for hours on end coding and writing software if they didn't believe they were creating something great.

---

[8] Fadell, Tony. Build. HarperCollins, 2022.
[9] Id at p15

But I also wonder whether the people who were cooped up in that building creating the software had real-world experience. Specializing in following a narrow course is not the map to success unless real-world experience says that you're creating a solution that will address someone's pain point.

When it comes to real-world experience, the generalist brings that to the table. The generalist has experienced more of what the world has to offer; the generalist can help every company avoid myopia.

One or the Other. Or Both!

Given that the multidisciplinary person is one who lives a wider, more learning-focused life, it follows that generalists should be more adaptable in leadership roles. Being a successful generalist involves having a broad education in multiple disciplines and recognizing how those disciplines converge in everyday actions. It can lead to greater creativity, innovation, and happiness.

One of the main advantages of being a generalist is the ability to see connections and patterns that specialists may miss. Because generalists have a wider range of experience and knowledge, they are more likely to recognize the relevance of ideas and insights from different fields, leading to more creative and innovative solutions to problems, as well as new ideas for products and services.

Another benefit is the ability to adapt to changing circumstances. Generalists are often better equipped to do this because they have more flexible and adaptable mindsets. They are used to dealing with new challenges and can draw on a range of experiences and skills to find solutions.

There is also evidence to suggest that being a generalist is beneficial for personal development and well-being. By pursuing a wide range of interests and activities, generalists are more likely to experience a sense of fulfillment and purpose and are less likely to feel stuck in a rut or trapped in a particular career or lifestyle.

One of the key proponents of this view is David Epstein, author of *Range: Why Generalists Triumph in a Specialized World*. Epstein makes the case that, in many fields, generalists are better equipped to succeed than specialists. He draws on a wide range of examples, from musicians and athletes to scientists and business leaders, to provide a compelling argument for the value of being a generalist. He argues that in order to succeed in today's world, individuals need to have a range of experiences and skills, rather than just deep expertise in one area. He cites numerous examples of successful individuals who started out in one field but who were able to transfer their skills and knowledge to another in order to achieve success. He also cites research showing that individuals with a broad range of experiences and skills are more likely to come up with innovative and creative solutions to problems.

The Message of Marshall McLuhan

Marshall McLuhan was a Canadian philosopher and media theorist who is best known for his work on the effects of media on society. He argued that media are not just tools for communication, but that they also shape the way we think and perceive the world. He famously argued that "The medium is the message", meaning that the medium through which a message is conveyed is just as important as the message itself.

From McLuhan's perspective, a holistic view is valuable because it allows individuals to see the world through multiple media, rather than just one. This means that generalists are better equipped to understand the ways in which different media shape our thinking and perception of the world. They are also more likely to be able to see through the biases and assumptions that are inherent in any particular medium.

For example, a specialist might be inclined to view the world through the lens of their particular field. They might see everything through the narrow focus of their area of expertise and be blind to the ways in which other fields shape the world. A generalist, on the other hand, is more likely to be able to see the world through multiple lenses. They might be able to see how the media shapes the way we think about politics, how technology changes the way we communicate, and how art shapes our cultural values.

Being a generalist allows individuals to make more informed decisions in all areas—whether in their personal relationships, their health and wellness, or their finances, having a broad range of knowledge and skills can help them make better decisions and avoid costly mistakes.

Adaptability and Agility in Leaders

In their 2020 book *Radical Uncertainty: Decision-Making Beyond the Numbers*, John Kay and Mervyn King argue that the modern world is characterized by complexity, ambiguity, and uncertainty. In such a world, specialization is no longer enough to cope with the challenges we face. Instead, we need to cultivate a new kind of mindset—one that values generalization over specialization.

According to Kay and King, generalists are individuals who possess a broad range of knowledge, skills, and experiences. They are comfortable dealing with complexity and ambiguity because they are used to working across different domains and disciplines. They are also adaptable and flexible, able to learn new things quickly, and apply their knowledge in creative ways. Generalists, therefore, are well-suited to thrive in an uncertain world. They can see the big picture, connect the dots, and come up with innovative solutions to complex problems. They are also good at working in teams, as they can bring different perspectives and experiences to the table.

An analysis of Kay and King's work suggests that generalists are particularly valuable in today's economy where the pace of change is rapid and unpredictable. In such an environment, specialization can become a liability, as it can lead to narrow-mindedness and a reluctance to adapt. Generalists, on the other hand, are always learning and growing, which makes them more resilient and adaptable.

The Decision Makers

In *The Signal and the Noise: Why So Many Predictions Fail—but Some Don't*, Nate Silver, a statistician and founder of FiveThirtyEight, a website that provides data-driven journalism on politics, economics, and sports, explores the world of prediction, examining the art and science of forecasting across a range of fields, from finance and sports to politics and weather. The central thesis of his book is that we live in an age of information overload, where data is abundant but the signal is often obscured by noise. Silver argues that the key to making better predictions is to distinguish between what is truly valuable information and what is just background noise.

Silver highlights the significance of considering probabilities and understanding how uncertainty influences our decisions. He stresses the importance of staying open-minded and adjusting our beliefs when new information emerges.

Fine Tuning the Decision

A central idea he presents is *Bayesian thinking*. This method means that instead of simply depending on past experiences or gut feelings, you adjust or refine your beliefs when you encounter new evidence. By adopting this Bayesian approach, Silver believes individuals can make more precise forecasts compared to using other methods.

Think of a leader in the middle of setting a direction or making a decision. Now imagine that leader has his or her hand on a dial. The wheel can be spun in one direction or the other as information becomes available. As leaders spin the dial, information and knowledge are filtered as the dial eventually comes to rest on a specific decision. That adjustment is a result of the knowledge and guidance that the leader has received during his or her life.

Multidisciplinary leaders have been inundated with knowledge from different directions throughout their lives. They have become masters at walking in multiple lanes. They have become adept at using Bayesian methods even though they may never realize it. Being able to have a 30,000-foot view of what is happening in the current moment makes them more ready to foster a culture of multidisciplinary collaboration, and they can leverage the insights and perspectives of people from different backgrounds to drive innovation and solve complex problems.

Someone with a vast array of knowledge is more likely to possess the willingness to embrace diversity and to create an environment where people feel comfortable sharing their ideas. This type of leadership requires a certain level of vulnerability and a willingness to admit it when you don't have all the answers. It also requires the ability to create a sense of psychological safety where people feel comfortable sharing their ideas without fear of judgment or retribution.

I spent many years in law enforcement as a prosecutor. The one thing that I was always certain of was that no matter how good a lawyer or cop someone was, it did not translate into being a powerful leader. The people who knew the rules, and how to follow them, we're not flexible leaders. They had great difficulty dealing with events that were outside the realm of their experience or the scope of their knowledge. The people who made better leaders were the ones who were diverse.

Every one of my clients fared better because I had the capability to be more adaptable when problems arose. When a problem was unpredictable, the specialist mindset failed. It was my multi-lane education that allowed me to be a fox. Hedgehogs do fine when predictability and consistency are the norm, but they often flounder when a variable enters the scene and throws the path off kilter. It was my multiple careers and avocations that allowed me to solve problems quicker. I knew when to challenge assumptions, and I also recognized the value of accepting reality. (Once again, my high school guidance counsellor was wrong.)

I was a specialist at criminal law, and my clients placed their lives in my hands, but it was my multidisciplinary training and my various other careers that allowed me to make faster decisions; communicate better with the courts, the jury, and other lawyers; and understand my clients better. It was the versatility and adaptability of a wider life that allowed me to be more effective.

In Isaiah Berlin's essay, he identified a few writers who were hedgehogs but wanted to be foxes and vice versa. In his conclusion, he determined that Tolstoy was basically both: "Tolstoy was by nature a fox but believed in being a hedgehog; that his gifts and achievement are one thing, and his beliefs, and consequently his interpretation of his own achievement, another."[10]

---

[10] Berlin, Isaiah, The Hedgehog and the Fox: An Essay on Tolstoy's View of History, Princeton University Press, 2013

Dare to Cross-Pollinate

Whether we're a specialist or a generalist depends on what we're doing. They aren't mutually exclusive. I know several generalists who are specialists in specific areas and many specialists who are generalists in other areas. The key to being a successful generalist is to have a broad education across multiple disciplines while recognizing how those disciplines converge in our everyday actions.

My multidisciplinary mindset is based on the idea that one person who dares to cross-pollinate several disciplines will be a driving force for innovation. This approach means that one individual can be the catalyst that leads to the creation of new and unexpected solutions. This is highlighted by one final example: Frank Gehry. Gehry is a renowned architect, artist, and designer, who made a name for himself as a multidisciplinary innovator. Born in Canada in 1929, Gehry has spent his career pushing the boundaries of traditional architecture and design, and his works can be found all over the world.

One of the things that sets Gehry apart as a multidisciplinary innovator is his ability to draw inspiration from a wide range of sources. He has always been interested in art and sculpture, and he has incorporated those interests into his architecture in unique and fascinating ways. His works are known for their fluidity and movement, often incorporating unusual materials, such as titanium and chain link.

In addition to his work in architecture, Gehry has also designed furniture, jewelry, and even clothing. He has worked with companies like Tiffany & Co. and Knoll to create innovative and unique designs that blend art and functionality in exciting new ways. His furniture designs are known for their playful and whimsical qualities, and they have been displayed in museums across the globe.

As of this writing, Gehry is 94 and continues to innovate and experiment with new materials and techniques, his work an inspiration to artists, architects, and designers everywhere. His ability to draw inspiration from a wide range of sources and to create works that are both functional and beautiful is a testament to his creativity and vision. His work continues to inspire and excite people and he will undoubtedly be remembered as one of the greatest innovators of our time.

Gehry embodies the multidisciplinary mindset and the idea that when people from different fields come together, they can create new ideas and innovations that would not have been possible otherwise. People from different fields bring different perspectives, experiences, and expertise to the table. When these perspectives are combined, they can lead to breakthrough ideas and new approaches to problem-solving.

JOURNEY MILEPOSTS

- **Weight of Expectation:** Think about the law school graduate's interaction at the beginning of this chapter. How do societal and familial expectations shape our individual paths and sense of self-worth? How might these pressures constrain our ability to see beyond the 'one big thing' and appreciate the multifaceted nature of life and its myriad opportunities?

- **The Dynamics of Adaptability vs. Expertise:** Reflect on the dichotomy between the fox and the hedgehog. In your personal and professional life, do you lean more towards being a fox or a hedgehog? Can one transition from being predominantly one to the other? How do you perceive the balance between depth (specialization) and breadth (generalization) in today's rapidly changing world?

- **Championing Diversity of Thought:** As highlighted in the discussion about workplaces seeking both specialists and generalists, ponder the significance of nurturing a diverse environment of thinkers. How can you, in your role, ensure that a balanced blend of both perspectives is always at play? And more fundamentally, how might you challenge yourself to remain open, adaptable, and perpetually curious, even when faced with the certainty of experts?

- **The Balance of Specialization and Generalization:** Theodore Levitt's "Marketing Myopia" underlines the danger of viewing one's industry too narrowly, which has led once-thriving sectors to stagnate. Think about your own profession or the industries you interact with daily. Where do you see the balance between the deep expertise of specialization and the broad vision of generalization? Is it more beneficial to have a laser-focused expertise in one area or to be a jack of all trades? Why?

- **Adaptability in a World of Constant Change:** Tony Fadell's journey with the groundbreaking Sony Magic Link illuminates the notion that sometimes being ahead of your time can be just as detrimental as being behind. With that in mind, consider the role of adaptability and timing. How important is it for leaders and innovators to be forward-thinking but also in sync with the present needs and readiness of society?

- **The Fox vs. the Hedgehog:** Drawing inspiration from Isaiah Berlin's essay and the author's personal experience in law enforcement, reflect on your own approach to problem-solving and adaptability. Do you identify more as a fox, who sees a multitude of strategies and paths, or a hedgehog, who moves with a single-focused approach? Moreover, how do both of these archetypes fit into today's multidimensional world?

- **The Essence of a Multidisciplinary Mindset:** What areas of expertise or disciplines intrigue you the most? Imagine combining your primary field with another discipline you're passionate about. What innovative ideas or solutions could emerge from such a fusion? Consider the impact that a multidisciplinary approach could have on your personal or professional life. Are there barriers preventing you from embracing such a mindset? Remember, by daring to cross-pollinate ideas, you're setting the stage for innovation and the creation of the unimaginable.

7

The Brain: Debunking Myths and Maximizing Potential

*The Brain—is wider than the Sky—
For—put them side by side—
The one the other will contain.*
— Emily Dickinson

Decision makers must have a multidisciplinary background to navigate the complexities of our modern world. For example, an engineer with a background in economics may be better equipped to make decisions about infrastructure projects, as they can consider the economic impact of the project as well as its engineering requirements.

Debunking the Myth

But what about that whole left brain/right brain discussion? We hear people say it all the time: "I can't do math; I'm too right brained" or "I'm no good at painting; I'm a left-brained person."

The idea that people learn—or think—with either their left or right hemisphere has been popular for many years. It suggests that some of us are more logical and analytical, while others are more creative and intuitive.

This popular belief oversimplifies the complexity of brain functions. It's time to set the record straight.

Historically, this myth may have originated from the association of the right hand being positive and the left hand being sinister. In many societies, the right hand is used for eating and greeting, and the left is used for hygiene (use your imagination). In theater, villains traditionally enter from the left. In fact, in Latin, the word for left is *sinistram*, from which the English *sinister* is derived.

A Brain Divided, but Not Against Itself

Studies have found that the brain is a complex organ that works as a whole. While certain regions of the brain may be more active during certain tasks, both hemispheres are involved in every aspect of learning and cognition.[1] In fact, research suggests that people learn best when both hemispheres of the brain are engaged, and that that when people are exposed to new information, their brain processes it in a way that integrates both analytical and creative thinking.

Your brain is divided into two parts, each side responsible for different things, like language and visualization. But they work together. While some individuals may have preferences

---

[1] Corballis, M. C. (2014). Left brain, right brain: Facts and fantasies. PLoS Biology, 12(1), e1001767. https://doi.org/10.1371/journal.pbio.1001767

for certain types of learning, it's essential to understand that this does not imply dominance of one hemisphere over the other. The brain seamlessly integrates both hemispheres when processing new information, combining analytical and creative thinking. While some think individuals can be either left-brain or right-brain dominant based on their personality and how they think, science hasn't found enough evidence to support this idea.

Harmonizing Both Sides

To study the right-brain/left-brain theory, scientists used a scan to examine the brains of 1011 people between the ages of 7 and 29.[2] They looked at how different parts of the brain on one side talked to each other, and how this differed from the way the parts of the brain on the other side communicated.

They found that, at any given time, there were certain hubs, or groups of brain regions, that were more active on either the left or the right side. The hubs on the left were responsible for things like daydreaming and language, while the hubs on the right were responsible for things like attention and focus.

They also found that the left and right hubs connected to each other in different ways, forming two separate networks, and that the connections within each network were stronger than the connections between the two. For example, when people are learning to read, both the left and right hemispheres

---

[2] Nielsen, J. A., Zielinski, B. A., Ferguson, M. A., Lainhart, J. E., & Anderson, J. S. (2013). An evaluation of the left-brain vs. right-brain hypothesis with resting state functional connectivity magnetic resonance imaging. PLoS ONE, 8(8), e71275. https://doi.org/10.1371/journal.pone.0071275

are active. The left hemisphere is responsible for processing the phonetic sounds of words, while the right hemisphere is involved in processing the visual aspects of written language.

Another example is when people are learning to play a musical instrument. The left hemisphere processes the logical aspects of music, such as rhythm and timing, while the right hemisphere processes the emotional and creative aspects.

It's clear that some people may have a natural preference for certain types of learning. Some may be more comfortable with logical and analytical thinking, while others are more inclined toward creative and intuitive thinking. This does not mean, however, that one hemisphere of the brain is more dominant than the other. The brain works as a whole to process new information. The brain dynamically adapts to various tasks, drawing from both analytical and creative resources. This adaptability is a significant benefit of adopting a multidisciplinary mindset.

The Multidisciplinary Advantage

As a decision-maker, it's essential to recognize the value of a multidisciplinary mind. Embracing diverse fields of knowledge and experiences allows you to make more well-rounded decisions. A multidisciplinarian isn't constrained by the limitations of a single discipline or the false belief in left-brain/right-brain dominance.

The human brain is a remarkable organ capable of adapting to any task. By actively seeking out diverse perspectives, disciplines, and experiences, you can enhance your ability to think critically, make informed decisions, and harness the full potential of your cognitive abilities.

While the left-brain/right-brain myth may persist in popular culture, it's important to recognize that the brain operates as a unified whole, combining analytical and creative thinking to tackle the multifaceted challenges we face.

The multidisciplinary mindset is a flagship of adaptability and cognitive versatility. By appreciating the interconnectedness of various disciplines, we can harness the full potential of our cognitive abilities and make informed, well-rounded decisions.

Multidisciplinarians don't fall back on excuses that say they can't do something because their brain *isn't wired that way*. Their brain *is* wired that way and they know it. The human brain is wired to accomplish any task we set before it. We only have to make the effort. The next time you think you can't do something because one side of your brain or the other won't work, stop it. Stop making excuses and grow.

JOURNEY MILEPOSTS

- **Multidisciplinary Decision Making:** Reflect on instances in your life where having knowledge from diverse disciplines could have aided in better decision-making. How might combining fields of knowledge, like engineering principles with economic understanding, as mentioned in the text, play a pivotal role in holistic decision-making in other areas of your life or work?

- **Challenging Prevailing Myths:** The left-brain/right-brain theory, despite being debunked, remains p revalent in many societal conversations. Why do you think certain myths, despite being scientifically disproven, continue to hold traction in popular culture? How can awareness of the true nature of brain functions empower individuals to overcome self-imposed limitations?

- **Harmony and Adaptability of the Brain:** The research discussed in this chapter highlights the brain's adaptability and how different hemispheres collaborate for various tasks. Think about how you can apply this knowledge to your personal and professional growth. Are there areas where you've pigeonholed yourself based on perceived strengths or weaknesses? How can understanding the brain's true nature challenge these beliefs?

- **The Power of the Multidisciplinary Mindset:** With the understanding that our brains are inherently equipped to handle tasks across disciplines, how might society benefit if more individuals cultivated a multidisciplinary mindset? What steps can you personally take to embrace diverse fields of knowledge and experiences, and thereby unlock the full potential of your cognitive abilities?

8

Jack of All Trades: A More Elastic Mind

*A jack of all trades is a master of none,
but oftentimes better than a master of one.*
— Unknown

Every one of my chapters starts with a notable quotation. I like quotes because they preserve the genius of the ages. If you ignored the quote above, read it again. It is not the version you know.

People always ask how you start writing a book. People have said, *I just start writing and see where it leads me.* Not me. Truthfully, I start in the middle and grow outward. I tell you this because this is the first chapter I wrote. I share that with you, so you understand the importance of shedding the fear that a Jack of all trades is a master of none. We are masters of integration.

Why the Bad Rap?

The negative connotation developed in the 20th century. The *Jack of all trades* is someone who dabbles in several areas and knows them superficially. *Master of none* was added to make the statement seem derogatory, which is a shame because the original, shorter version celebrated those who could do lots of things and do them well. It described those who were good at integrating all their skills and knowledge to solve problems and fix things, and who were unafraid to try new things and learn more about different fields.

Originally, Jack of all trades "… was a term of praise, rather than disparagement, as it is today.[1]" In *Morris Dictionary of Word and Phrase Origins,* William and Mary Morris wrote, "One writer noted 'Old Lewis' was sort of 'Jack of all trades,' which made the rest of the tradesmen jealous. 'Jack,' in those days, was a generic term for 'man.'[2]"

The concept first appeared in print in English writer Geffray Minshull's *Essays and Characters of a Prison.*[3] Minshull, while in the king's prison for debt, wrote of the various people he met there. He opined that the man who greeted him at the gates of the prison was a Jack-of-all-trades. He was impressed with the man, so as Minshull sat in prison, he assigned the man the various roles he suspected he played in life.

Interestingly enough, the first negative connotation in print was in 1592, when the writer Robert Greene dismissed William

---

[1] Morris, William, and Mary Morris, Morris Dictionary of Word and Phrase Origins. Harper Collins, 1988
[2] Morris, supra
[3] Minshull (Mynshul), Geffray, Essays and Characters of A Prison, 1612

Shakespeare as "Johannes Factorum." The word *factorial* was used to describe a leader who had many diverse activities or responsibilities so, in essence, Greene labeled Shakespeare a "Johnny Do All." Even though he meant the label as a put-down, it's worth noting that Robert Greene is largely forgotten while Shakespeare lives on. Greene's intended insult did not stand the test of time.

The Jack allows the knowledge of diverse trades to benefit the community. This person can fix things, resolve problems, and is a master of integration, seeing the world differently than those who specialize. The *Jack of all trades* is a generalist.

Leonardo da Vinci was a Jack of all trades, perhaps the most famous multidisciplinarian in history. Born in 1452, da Vinci was an artist, inventor, scientist, and engineer, among many other things. His diverse interests and expertise allowed him to make significant contributions to a wide range of fields, and his legacy continues to inspire and influence us. As an artist, he is renowned for his paintings, including the famous *Mona Lisa* and *The Last Supper*. He was a master of technique, and his paintings are characterized by their lifelike realism and attention to detail. But da Vinci's talents extended far beyond the realm of art. He was also a skilled inventor and engineer, credited with designing everything from flying machines to submarines. His scientific studies included investigations into anatomy, optics, geology, and other fields.

Da Vinci's cross-disciplinary approach was a product of his insatiable curiosity and desire to understand the world around him. He approached each new challenge with an open mind, bringing his diverse skills and knowledge to bear on the problem at hand. His ability to see connections and relationships between different disciplines allowed him to come up with innovative solutions and ideas that were ahead of his time.

As the world becomes increasingly complex and interconnected, individuals like da Vinci serve as a reminder of the power and potential of a multidisciplinary approach to problem-solving and innovation.

Unfortunately, many of us have been encouraged to specialize in just one thing, to be a *master of one,* but that's not the only way to succeed. In fact, I believe that generalists are the real MVPs of life. I encourage you to celebrate generalists and embrace why they're so important. But for now, let's focus on how they think. They're not limited by one field of knowledge, so they can approach problems from many angles. They're curious, always learning and exploring. They know more than one big thing.

Think Like a Fox

The knowledge and learning base of generalists is rather broad. They don't retreat to a single location of their minds to find answers. There are multiple avenues of knowledge they can reach into, and multiple streams of information are processed in their brains at any given time. Like a fox, *we know many things.* It is your thought process that taps into your network of diverse domains.

We've discussed several examples of well-known multi-disciplinary people, but how do they think? Let's look at the science.

Attention is an interesting creature. Sometimes we pay attention. Sometimes we don't. But, in the end, attention is how we survive, it's a cornerstone of our existence. Attention, memory, and perception are the gateways to problem solving, rational thought, irrational thought, and innovation. All those processes are the overlapping elements that contribute to our ability to be cognitive creatures. The cognitive process is a full sensory, intellectual, and emotional operation that defines our behavior.

Our brain receives information from multiple sources and directs our behavior according to the information that it processes. What we hear, see, touch, taste, and smell fuels the brain's decision making. The brain operates on both conscious and subconscious levels. Many times, we aren't fully aware of what information is flying at us, but our brain still acts upon it at lighting speed.

I recently bought a new Jeep Wrangler, all black, four doors, and I call it Pilar. Yes, I named it after Ernest Hemingway's boat. Okay, let's get back on track. The first time I got behind the wheel in Pilar I looked to the right of the steering column to find the ignition button. Upon starting her up, I reached with my left hand to open the window. Whoa! The buttons weren't there.

They were always right there in my Toyota Avalon. I drove Avalons for over twenty years. The window controls are on the door. Always. But, not in a Jeep. A Jeep's window controls are on the center console. So, I found them and opened the window. As I pulled out of the parking lot, it began to drizzle. I reached to turn on my headlights, and spayed washer fluid on my windshield. Yep, that's also different in a Jeep.

In my Avalon I never had to look for the ignition, I never looked for the window controls, and I certainly never sprayed my windshield with water when I turned on the headlights. I never actually thought about doing any of that. I just did it. Even though a series of actions was required to make the things happen, I didn't think about them. They happened subconsciously. I intuitively knew how to turn on the car, open the window, and turn on the headlights. But it wasn't always that way.

Just like in my Jeep, at one time I had to get used to certain actions in my Avalon. But after driving the same model of car for over twenty years, the actions became instincts. They were not a thought-out process. But in the Jeep, I still must look for everything and I'm 1200 miles in. Pilar hasn't trained me yet. I still have to pay *attention* if I want anything to happen. I can't shut off my conscious mind. Without my conscious mind, the car wouldn't even start. And yet, a couple weeks ago I jumped in my Avalon and I was halfway down my eight-hundred-foot driveway before I even realized I was driving. The car had become a part of me.

Scientifically, there are two systems of thought at play here. One is intuitive, the other is deliberative.

Call and Response

When listening to the blues you'll often hear something that is known as *call and response:* two musicians going back-and-forth as if having a conversation. The first guitarist will play a piece of music, *a call.* Then the second guitarist, hearing that call, plays *a response.* Sometimes the response is a continuation of the call, sometimes it's complementary, and sometimes it's a contrasting reply. Human cognition is much like that. We receive an external stimulus and we respond accordingly. Sometimes the response is intuitive or instinctive, and other times we have to think about it and consciously compose it. Our degree of knowledge and level of skill may influence the creation of our response.

Labelling the two systems of thinking as *System 1* and *System 2*[4] is adopted from the work of Keith E. Stanovich & Richard F. West.[5] They defined System 1 as automatic, largely unconscious, and relatively undemanding of computational capacity. System 2 typified controlled processing, the processes of analytic intelligence.[6]

Daniel Kahneman, recipient of the Nobel Prize in economics, breaks down the dual-modal thinking process by identifying System 1 as operating automatically and quickly, with very little sense of effort or voluntary control. On the other hand, he frames System 2 as us being ourselves. He states that, "System

---

[4] Kahneman, Daniel. Thinking, Fast and Slow. Farrar, Straus and Giroux, 2011.
[5] Stanovich, K., & West, R. (2000). Individual differences in reasoning: Implications for the rationality debate? Behavioral and Brain Sciences, 23(5), 645-665. doi:10.1017/S0140525X00003435
[6] Id., at 658

2 is the conscious reasoning self that has beliefs, makes choices, and decides what to think about and what to do."[7]

So, in short order, it was System 1 that allowed me to get into my Toyota Avalon and hit the road with ease. I didn't have to think about it. Whether it be through prior experience, muscle memory, or my subconscious, I operated my Toyota Avalon without a thought. On the other hand, my Jeep Wrangler still demands that System 2 step up and tell me what to do. It hasn't yet become instinct.

When I first drove the Avalon I had the same problems. But, over time, my System 2 abilities reprogrammed the way my System 1 works. By reprogramming what would normally be an automatic function of attention and memory, a System 2 task became a System 1 task. The operation of the vehicle became instinct. Therefore, it's only a matter of time (I hope!) until driving my Jeep Wrangler will be done by System 1.

However, it's not at all likely that operating the vehicle will be completely surrendered by my System 2 mind. I will always need to pay attention when driving. Which is probably why my youngest daughter, when she was six, would say, "Don't drive with your eyes closed." Good advice for both System 1 and System 2 processes.

Think about yourself as you drive a vehicle. There are functions of the operation that are clearly intuitive and instinctive, like pressing the accelerator or opening the window. You may sing along with your favorite song as it plays on the sound system. I'm not talking about a song where you have to think

---
[7] Kahneman, Id at p20-21

about the lyrics, I'm talking about one where you know the lyrics by heart and you are ready to karaoke. For some of us it might be Queen's "We Are the Champions", for others it might be Harry Styles's "As It Was". Whatever the song, you can't help but sing it aloud. But then, in the middle of the song, a car swerves in front of you as the traffic light turns red. You slam the brakes. You still hear the song but your voice went silent. Your attention was redirected to the road ahead of you. You may not have known it, but your brain had been working to remember the lyrics. System 2 was fully operational. It was sending the words to your mouth one after another and then, that fast, it stopped. Your attention was diverted. Your mind focused on the almost-accident. Your mind fully came together and told your body to stop the car as soon as possible.

Paying attention is an energy dump. The minute you must pay attention your resources drop and you're unable to perform at your peak. Kahneman refers to such a situation as *going beyond your budget*. You used up all your attention. The nature of an effortful activity is that it drains your mental resources.

There you have it. Next time you catch yourself daydreaming or just going through the motions, that's System 1. And when you're solving a math problem or trying to figure out a complex issue, that's System 2. It's like having two brains in one! Being aware of this can really affect the way we think and make decisions. So let's appreciate both our intuitive and thinking minds, and keep widening our horizons so we can operate in multiple lanes.

If Only It Were That Simple...

Attention, memory, and perception are crucial to our existence. They're the gateway to problem-solving, rational and irrational thought, and innovation. And the brain's decision-making process is fueled by what we hear, see, touch, taste, and smell. Our conscious and subconscious minds work together to process all that information and guide our behavior.

Since I don't purport to be a scientist, I am not really concerned about the labels. Suffice it to say that the two systems operate hand-in-hand, and I am not giving preference to either one. Both systems are necessary for our survival. In this book, I'm looking at the two systems so we can improve our System 1 by widening our horizons so that more and more of our actions and thoughts become natural because of the multiple lanes in which we operate.

Looking back at the blues guitarist, a skilled, experienced musician will respond instinctively because the music is a language they fully understand. Someone like me, who is new to the game and only moderately proficient at understanding musical scales, has to engage in System 2 thinking to make sure that the fingers are in the right places on the fretboard. It is work.

If you're reading this book as an English-speaking person, the words are easy to follow and understand. Si, se lo scrivessi in italiano, il tuo processo mentale passerebbe immediatamente al Sistema 2 e si spegnerebbe. Ti congelerai. (Yes, I wrote this in Italian. Unless you know the language your thought process immediately switched to System 2.)

So let's look at System 1 as an intuitive/instinctive function and System 2 as a function of thinking/effort.

When we consider a specialist, maybe a surgeon, the skills and talents they learned throughout their lifetime are honed and polished. Performing a delicate operation becomes a function of instinct, but the thinking mind is on high alert, providing the backup for everything the surgeon does. Paying attention to the heart monitor, the blood pressure, the location of the incision. Every step in the process occurs naturally at the fingertips through muscle memory, but the mind pays very close attention so the fingertips don't make a mistake.

Let's face it, we want a surgeon whose hands are as steady as possible, one whose hands know what to do. But we also want that surgeon to be fully aware of the risks and maintain vigilance and watch to make sure that none of the risks occur. We want a specialist. Or do we?

When my first daughter was born it was touch and go. My wife was in labor, but the baby wasn't coming. Olivia refused to leave the womb. They did an EKG and monitored the baby. Suddenly, everyone panicked. We were told that the cord was likely wrapped around her neck. It was time for an emergency C-section. As the doctors and nurses prepared, they stationed a nurse outside the room to tell anyone who entered, "They are both lawyers." A bit frustrated and scared, I stepped into the hallway, looked at the nurse, and said and, "I can hear you."

They rushed my wife into surgery. The cord was, in fact, around the baby's neck. The C-section was clearly warranted. After the operation I got to hold Olivia for a second or two, then they took her away for examination. Then a doctor arrived who I have since named Dr. Frankenstein. He was tall, pale-faced, and emotionless. He told us that Olivia's temperature had spiked, and that it was bad. He used the phrase, "…sometimes this can be fatal. Her temperature is very high."

Then he turned and left with the same slow, empty strut with which he had entered. I turned to the nurse. She looked like a deer in the headlights. She said, "He is the best neonatal doctor we have on staff. Um, I don't think her temperature is out of the norm. She'll be okay."

I told her I didn't care if he was the best neonatal doctor on staff. I asked her who was the *second*-best neonatal doctor on staff.

About twenty minutes later we met another doctor who said she was monitoring Olivia, that she should be okay, and that we should be prepared for her to stay for a couple of days. And then she discussed her experience and her thoughts as to why Olivia would be fine. We were greatly relieved. This second-best doctor saved my daughter's life and allowed my wife to start breathing again.

Sure, this doctor also was a specialist, but we later learned that she was a grade-school soccer coach and had various other specialties and skills that gave her a much more human appeal.

For her, the ability to communicate with the children on her soccer team, and as a more broadly skilled individual, allowed her to speak humanly. She wasn't afraid to live in multiple lanes and still excel in her primary role.

Being a grade-school coach, refereeing games, and being a mother have nothing to do with medicine. But they have everything to do with being aware of humans, making decisions, and the ability to think on your feet. She had a much better System 1, or intuitive, processing system. For her, communication was natural. It wasn't a deliberative or laborious process. When she spoke to me, all her lanes were perfectly integrated, and our conversation showed her flawless integration.

Dr Frankenstein, on the other hand, had no other lanes to drive in.

On a sidenote, I went down to the cafeteria to grab something to eat, since my stomach was calmer now, and shared a table with Dr. Frankenstein. I won't elaborate upon our conversation, but I'm sure that even today, thirty years later, he never wants to see me again. He spent far too much time practicing medicine and not enough time living a life. His experience was way too narrow to allow him to talk to humans. He had no other lanes of experience to work in.

Calling the Lawyer

When I was a lawyer, I eschewed free initial consultations. That was the norm in the industry for criminal defense lawyers. Get the people in the door, give them a free initial consultation, and then quote your fees. Not for me.

I charged people when they came in my door, but not because I was a money-grubbing lawyer. The opposite was true. I cared about my clients.

When a client explains their problem—they got arrested for this, they got arrested for that—the instinct of a defense lawyer is to immediately jump to a conclusion that benefits the defense of the client. In the beginning, that's what I did. I listened to the client, jumped to a conclusion, and framed their defense. I quickly found out that this isn't beneficial to the client or to my reputation.

My discovery originated with the construction of my home. Having been a civil engineer, I designed my own home, did most of the blueprints, hired my general contractor, and supervised its construction. My engineering background was finally being used for a rather big and personal project. Everything I knew about construction and building materials came into play. From the concrete foundation to the roof framing, everything we did was done for a very good reason: I wanted the house to withstand the test of time. I had spent enough money to know I wasn't going to be moving out any time soon. Therefore, I couldn't afford to have it fall down around me.

Every stud, every floor joist, and every electrical line was placed in a very specific position to make sure that the house would remain functional and solid well into the future. We didn't have the ability to make assumptions and do guesswork. Everything had to be calculated to ensure it was correct. Engineering is probably one of the most detailed tasks the deliberative cognitive mind can do. You don't do engineering by guesswork. And, frankly, even though there are some things where assumptions are allowable, I hadn't practiced enough engineering to make guesses.

In law we talk about circumstantial evidence, evidence that is inferred by the facts of the case so that it makes something more or less true. The adage is, "If it walks like a duck and talks like a duck, it's probably a duck." In construction, it might look like an eight-foot stud, it might feel like an eight-foot stud, but when you take out the tape measure and it measures 95 inches, it's only a 7'11" stud. That doesn't work.

The breakthrough was when I realized that this thought process, the calculations of the engineer, was extremely valuable to me in my law practice. My clients deserved more than my assumptions. See, when you do a free initial consultation, you're racing against the clock. Time is money and lawyers bill by the hour. The pressure is on to get the client in and out as fast as possible and collect a retainer.

By charging my client for the initial, I knew they would get the full hour. I also knew that I could focus on them rather than on some other client whose retainer was in the bank. There were many times when a client would tell me they had already seen another lawyer. Then they would tell me how that lawyer told them they had a defense. That was always a difficult hurdle to jump because I had to explain that the lawyer had made assumptions about the facts of the case. In the rush to get the client out the door the lawyer heard what they needed to hear or asked just enough questions to get the client to have faith in their representation, and then asked for the retainer. I wouldn't do that. I saw building my client's case as if I were building a house. It wasn't about guesswork. It wasn't about making assumptions. It was about identifying the correct materials to build a solid defense.

Engineering and law are clearly two different lanes, but they worked together for me and allowed me to become a very good defense lawyer. And it goes without saying that being a lawyer helped me as an engineer because I negotiated some pretty good contracts with my subcontractors. Honestly, that's really not an integration of lanes. It's more of a fortuitous circumstance. This blending of my careers is not unusual. It is only a sample. The ability to analyze a situation without jumping to conclusions is the result of experience.

As we process information, System 2 processes what we know and seeks answers to the questions that arise. When we work in one lane we deprive ourselves of the observations and knowledge that other lanes offer. It's the uncertainties that cause us to assign probabilities, subconsciously or consciously, to whether something is true, could happen, or may happen. The unknown unknown is what John Kay and Mervyn King call *Radical Uncertainty*.[8]

We'll explore decision making later, but for now I would suggest that multi-disciplinary knowledge improves the accuracy of our decisional heuristics. It alleviates cognitive load and burnout. It makes for less exhaustion and less work, helping us avoid irrational or inaccurate conclusions. The faster we are capable of changing lanes the less inaccuracies and biases

---

[8] Kay, John, and Mervyn King. Radical Uncertainty: Decision-Making beyond the Numbers. W.W. Norton & Company, 2021.

interfere with our System 1 reactions and, subsequently, our System 2 analysis.

As we assess situations and act appropriately, as we amass a broader spectrum of talents, knowledge, and skills, the more powerful our analytic abilities in the System 2 cognitive realm become. Simultaneously, we will have better control over our System 1 reactions.

The Jack of All Trades: Mastering the Dual-Thought System

In the intricate dance of cognition and problem-solving, System 1 and System 2 thinking play pivotal roles. While many navigate these two cognitive systems in relative isolation, depending on their professional or personal leanings, the jack of all trades emerges as a unique figure who seamlessly interweaves the instinctual with the analytical. This ability to marry intuition with deliberation allows the generalist to harness the strengths of both cognitive systems and employ them in a synergistic fashion.

Fluid Mastery of Reflexive Thought

The generalist's diverse array of experiences equips them with an enriched System 1, the intuitive, fast-acting facet of our cognitive processes. Their broad spectrum of knowledge and exposure means they can instinctually react to a vast range of situations, drawing upon an extensive reservoir of past experiences and insights. This rich tapestry of memories, shaped by various disciplines, allows for quick, automatic judgments and responses that are often surprisingly accurate.

Moreover, the Jack of all trades is not just confined to their immediate field of expertise but can instinctively understand and relate to a variety of scenarios and contexts. This enhanced intuitive processing, enriched by their multidisciplinary experiences, positions them to recognize patterns and connections that might elude others.

Harmonizing the Systems

System 2, the deliberate, logical thinking, is where detailed analysis and conscious thought reside. It's no surprise that the generalist, given their diverse background, can switch to this mode of thinking with finesse. The Jack of all trades doesn't merely rely on instinct; they're adept at diving deep, analyzing situations meticulously, and employing a multidisciplinary lens to find solutions.

The generalist's ability to think critically across multiple domains offers them a broader perspective. This width of understanding, combined with the depth of analytical thought from System 2, means they can dissect problems from multiple angles, often leading to innovative solutions that draw upon diverse fields of knowledge.

Integration: Where System 1 Meets System 2

What truly sets the Jack of all trades apart is their exceptional skill at integrating the automatic, instinctual responses of System 1 with the methodical, analytical approaches of

System 2. They fluidly transition between gut reactions and in-depth analysis, ensuring their decisions are both rapid and well-informed.

In situations where time is of the essence, they can lean into their enriched System 1 for swift decisions. In scenarios demanding thorough scrutiny, their adept System 2 comes into play. However, it's often the fusion of both—where intuition is checked and refined by logical analysis—that the generalist truly shines, producing results that are both efficient and robust.

Jack of All Trades and a Master of Integration

The generalist's unique positioning at the crossroads of diverse disciplines makes them adept at leveraging both instinctual and analytical modes of thinking. In a world that often demands both speed and accuracy, the generalist, with their mastery over System 1 and System 2, emerges as a beacon of cognitive versatility and excellence.

The Jack of all trades epitomizes the very essence of integrated knowledge. Through the lens of this unique individual, the world is not a series of disjointed, unrelated phenomena but rather a fluid, dynamic continuum where each discipline informs and enriches the other. In the eyes of a generalist, the connections are not only clear but also intrinsic, illuminating pathways of understanding that might remain obscured to the specialist.

These connections are not happenstance; they are the product of a mind that has learned to see not just with a focused gaze but with a peripheral vision that encompasses a broader spectrum. The generalist thrives not in silos but in open fields of thought where ideas from various domains mingle, intersect, and sometimes clash, giving birth to innovative solutions and unprecedented insights.

Back to the Blues

When guitarists engage in a call-and-response musical interlude, the interchange is largely intuitive. The notes are spontaneous, but not random. The guitarist may appear to be delivering a random response, but she is actually well versed in musical scales and the musical key within the scales. The reaction appears to be spontaneous and intuitive. And it is because the guitarist has mastered the skills. The notes flow instinctively and naturally. This can be like System 1 thinking.

On the other hand, if the guitarist is writing a musical composition or does not consistently practice mastering the art, this is purely System 2. This is a deliberate, analytical, and slower, more considered approach.

What creates the most amazing pieces of music is when, during a live performance, the call ignites an immediate System 1-like reaction from the responder, sparking an organic musical conversation.

In a world teeming with information and knowledge from myriad disciplines, the Jack of all trades stands tall as the Master of Integration. Their ability to weave through different fields, drawing connections and insights, is not just a skill but a form of mastery that is both rare and invaluable.

The Jack of all trades embodies the cross-disciplinary lens that allows the same texture and dynamic as the beauty of call-and-response in the blues. Much like a seasoned musician, the fluid response of the well-versed and diversely skilled leader creates a harmony of rhythm with a melody of expression as they make decisions and work together with others.

JOURNEY MILEPOSTS

- **The Evolution of Perception:** The term *Jack of all trades* has gone from a commendation to a criticism, tracing back centuries in literature. Why do you think society's view of generalists has shifted, and what factors, in your opinion, have led to the negativity surrounding this title? Reflect on how various historical and social contexts might have influenced this evolution of perception, and consider if, in today's complex world, it might be time for another shift in perspective.

- **The Renaissance of Multidisciplinarity:** Leonardo da Vinci, a paragon of the Renaissance, embodied the essence of a multidisciplinarian. Reflect on how da Vinci's diverse knowledge across multiple fields contributed to his legendary legacy. As you progress through this book, think about how today's world mirrors the interconnectedness of the Renaissance era. In what ways can adopting a multidisciplinary approach be beneficial for problem-solving and innovation in contemporary times?

- **Integrated Expertise vs. Singular Specialization:** What areas of your life might benefit from integrating various "lanes" of experiences, to develop a more holistic and empathetic approach? Think about how specialists, while experts in their fields, might sometimes miss out on the broader human experience. Do you think being a generalist or a specialist with a wide range of experiences outside their specialization makes one more effective in their primary role? Why or why not?

- **Conscious vs. Subconscious Processes in Learning and Mastery:** Consider the story of driving the Toyota Avalon versus the Jeep Wrangler. In what areas of your life have you transitioned from needing conscious, deliberate thought (System 2) to intuitive, automatic action (System 1)? How did this shift occur? Moreover, reflect on the balance needed between these two systems when performing tasks or making decisions. How can we better train our System 2 to enrich and enhance our System 1 reactions, especially in areas where we wish to become experts or specialists?

- **Cognitive Versatility: A Beacon of Excellence:** The generalist is a master over both instinctual (System 1) and analytical (System 2) modes of thinking. How essential do you think this cognitive versatility is in navigating the complexities and ambiguities of the contemporary informational landscape? In what ways can the ability to switch between different cognitive modes enhance decision-making and adaptability in various professional and personal contexts?

- **The Fluid Dynamics of Disciplinary Integration:** Reflect on the portrayal of the generalist as someone who doesn't see the world as disjointed, unrelated phenomena, but rather a dynamic continuum where disciplines intermingle and enrich one another. How does this fluid, integrated approach to knowledge impact innovation and problem-solving in our rapidly changing world? Do you believe that cultivating a broader, more integrated perspective could lead to richer insights and more robust solutions in various fields of inquiry and practice?

9

Decision-Making: A Mosaic of Experiences

Expertise is not a single skill; it is a collection of skills, and the same professional may be highly expert in some of the tasks in her domain while remaining a novice in others.
— Daniel Kahneman

Life isn't seen through just one lens. It's a blend of the multiple lenses we choose to look through. Making decisions is a daily thing, whether you're running a startup, leading a company, or just living life. The more skills and know-how you gather from different fields, the better you get at seeing the full picture. It's like having a bunch of different camera lenses, each with its own special ability.

If you play soccer on the weekends, you will understand teamwork and strategy in a whole new light. If you allow it, the soccer mindset can totally level up how you make decisions for a group project at work or when planning a family trip. Each new skill or knowledge adds a new tool to your toolbox, and soon you're not just hammering away with one tool; you've got a whole toolkit helping you tackle life's challenges. And the best part? Every time you pull out a new tool, you're like, "Whoa, where'd that come from? What else have I got in here?"

The journey of learning and connecting the dots never really ends. Do you remember those really crazy "word problems" we used to get in grade school? The ones that had us all thinking, *Why on earth would I need to know this?* Well, you no longer need to calculate the speed at which trains travel between Ohio and California or worry about the number of eggs in a basket after Katie takes eight and Jan adds twelve and breaks two, but the whole thinking-behind-the-thinking thing? That's gold!

Those math riddles weren't just about numbers. They were about sizing up situations, piecing things together, and getting our brains to flex. Those skills aren't just for math. They're for life! So the next time you're puzzling over something, remember those nutty word problems. You might just find answers in the most unexpected nooks and crannies.

For example, a background in art will give someone a much more visual mindset. Being able to take a look at a problem and verbalize it becomes easier because it's much like painting a picture. The more we know the more we look for pieces of the puzzle to complete a view of a situation. The artist can visualize the missing information.

We all have the skills to visualize information, but how do we apply those skills when we see a problem? Maybe you're looking at the structure of a problem because you do woodworking, or you map the problem as you would a long-distance cycling route, or you're looking at the various components of the problem because you're a cook. We should look at all problems from the wider perspective of our lives rather than from the perspective of the lane we are in at the moment. Go wider. Think across disciplines.

Decision-making becomes easier if we rely upon our broad range of skills, knowledge, and experiences to holistically view a situation. Intentionally pulling pieces of the puzzle from other domains is how we internally build and strengthen our networks across disciplines. When it comes to decision-making, a multidisciplinary approach avoids the pitfall of solely relying on the immediately available information.

But be wary. Humans are prone to making biased decisions, whether we're aware of it or not. This tendency can lead to overlooking other relevant data or perspectives. And worse yet, we fall into the trap of making assumptions based on our past knowledge and experiences. We do this because of the way we unconsciously filter received information. Why? Because sometimes it's unconsciously just too much work to switch from System 1 to System 2 thinking.

I prefer to think of a bias as a cognitive shortcut: a faster but less informed route to a decision. Once someone engages their System 2 thinking, the more likely they will be to avoid jumping to conclusions and succumbing to bias. The ultimate goal is to recognize that you are seeing the problem through a filter, remove the filter, and see the situation for what it really is.

Everything We Think Changes What We See

A cognitive bias is a flaw in reasoning that causes us to misinterpret information and arrive at inaccurate conclusions. It happens because our brains are constantly bombarded with information from countless sources throughout the day. To cope with this influx of data, our brains develop ranking systems and shortcuts to help it prioritize and process information more efficiently. Unfortunately, these shortcuts and ranking systems aren't always objective because they're influenced by our unique life experiences.

These cognitive shortcuts are mental filters through which we perceive and interpret information based on our past experiences and beliefs. Our experiences, beliefs, and values all contribute to the way we perceive and interpret information resulting in us making a mental leap that can have serious implications in decision making.

The more we understand the potential cognitive shortcut, the more we are able to mitigate its adverse effect. The more widely we view the problem, the more we are willing to seek out alternative perspectives. Embracing a holistic approach is a powerful antidote to taking a shortcut. This is achieved through regular self-reflection, seeking out feedback from others, and actively searching for diverse viewpoints.

The Multidisciplinary Decision-Maker

When someone has conditioned themselves to be a lifelong learner, knowing one or two things is never enough. The harder and deeper someone digs, the more information they gain and the more likely they will overcome bias, because the more tools they will have in their tool kit. And more importantly, they will be more adept at using those tools. Also, a lifelong learner is more ready to dive in to learn more about the problem as they prepare to solve it.

One reason we take shortcuts is that attention is a limited resource. We simply can't evaluate every single detail and event when forming our thoughts and opinions. As a result, we often rely on mental shortcuts that speed our ability to make judgments, but that can also lead to bad assumptions.

A background in multiple fields can help us stop taking shortcuts in several ways.

- We are exposed to different perspectives and ways of thinking, which can challenge our pre-existing beliefs and broaden our understanding.

- We are trained to think critically and analyze information from different angles, helping us question assumptions and seek evidence that supports or contradicts our beliefs.

- Our experience in adjusting to different contexts and ways of thinking makes us more flexible and adaptable in our thinking, helping us to be open to new information and ideas.

- We often take a holistic approach to problem-solving, considering multiple factors and perspectives, which can help us overcome confirmation bias by considering a range of evidence and perspectives.

In short, a multidisciplinary background is a valuable asset in avoiding jumping to conclusions without fully considering all information.

The Multidisciplinary Antidote to Cognitive Biases

Cognitive shortcuts can lead us astray, causing us to make irrational judgments and decisions based on flawed or incomplete information. Let's examine several of these filters in more detail and take a look at the way a more holistic review changes impetus behind each shortcut.

As you go through the remaining parts of this chapter, we'll look into the various shortcuts that cloud our thinking. For each, we will comment on the ways a multidisciplinary approach may better equip you to navigate these pitfalls. Take a moment and think about each one as we discuss it. Ask yourself where it has appeared in your life.

Echo Chamber Effect

The Echo Chamber Effect gives more weight to information that confirms our existing beliefs. This shortcut causes people to favor information that supports what they already think or believe, while disregarding information that challenges those beliefs. Simply put, they echo what they already believe.

Some examples of this shortcut include paying attention to news sources that exclusively support your views, and refusing to listen to opposing arguments. By filtering out opposing views, we conserve mental resources and protect self-esteem, making us feel that our beliefs are accurate. Generally, this is a tendency to look for, interpret, and remember information that confirms pre-existing beliefs or ideas, while ignoring or discounting information that contradicts them, leading to poor decision-making and a distorted view of reality.

As an example of this effect, imagine that Bob believes that eating late at night leads to weight gain. Whenever he reads articles or hears stories that support this belief, he remembers them and cites them as truth. However, when he is confronted with studies that contradict his belief, he summarily dismisses them as outliers, flawed, or pure fraud. Simply put, he believes those pieces of information that support his belief and rejects all others.

Avoiding this shortcut is particularly challenging for those with a narrow or specialized background as they may be more likely to filter information through their particular lens or perspective. However, when we're able to pull ideas from our other lanes of travel and work, we can broaden our perspective and reduce the impact of confirmation bias.

For example, an individual with a background in psychology who is studying the effects of social media on mental health may be more likely to focus on psychological factors. But if they also have a background in sociology, they may be more likely to consider the social and cultural factors that contribute to the issue.

In addition to broadening perspective, a multidisciplinary background can also help individuals develop critical-thinking skills. Critical thinking involves evaluating information objectively and considering different viewpoints. With experience in multiple fields, we can practice these skills and learn to identify and challenge our own biases, helping us be more open to alternative viewpoints and less likely to engage in confirmation bias.

A multidisciplinary background is a valuable tool for avoiding the echo chamber effect. By broadening perspective and developing critical thinking skills, we can approach problems with a more open mind and make more objective evaluations of information.

I Knew It All Along!

It's said that hindsight is 20/20. When we look back on events, the evidence that they were predictable becomes clearer *after* they have occurred.

This shortcut leads people to believe they knew all along that something would happen, even if it was a random event, like insisting that you knew which political candidate would win an election or that you knew the answer to a question you got wrong on a test. The thing about this rear-view filter is that the belief is *real* to the individual. This occurs because of our ability to misremember past predictions, our tendency to view events as inevitable, and our belief that we could have foreseen certain developments. This effect can cause people to overestimate their ability to predict events, which may result in unwise risks moving forward.

Our mind takes this shortcut to help us avoid the complexity of the decision-making process and underestimate the degree of uncertainty involved in making predictions.

A cross-disciplinary thinker will readily recognize when this filter clouds their thinking. They look beyond and around the filter to see a situation or problem from various perspectives because that is what they do. By considering multiple viewpoints, we can avoid the trap of focusing through a cloudy filter and instead focus on a more comprehensive analysis of a situation.

As lifelong learners, we are unafraid of not knowing or not predicting. We're willing to accept our ignorance as a stepping-stone towards greater growth and learning. We naturally want to know, so we investigate. Everything is a potential learning opportunity.

First Impressions Last Forever

We are overly influenced by the first piece of information we hear (the anchor). This can have a significant impact on various aspects of our lives, from price negotiations to medical diagnoses.

Our minds get anchored on a specific piece of information, and we do not move from it. We become anchored to that first impression. So sometimes, when we meet someone, the first impression is the one we keep no matter what they do to change it.

Imagine you're in the market for a new iPhone. You see the first ad and the price is $1500. When you go to Apple's website, you realize you can lower the price by reducing memory or screen size, but you can't seem to pull the trigger because your first impression tells you that anything less than a $1500 model is not going to serve you. Everything else is second class.

The more lanes in which we live, and the more we learn about the world, the less likely we are to dig in and anchor to our first impression. The more you see the more you know, and the less likely we are to be instantly judgmental. Someone with a multidisciplinary background has been exposed to different perspectives, approaches, and ways of thinking, allowing them to always be curious and thus less likely to rely on the first piece of information they receive.

For example, someone with a background in psychology and economics may be able to recognize the psychological biases that affect decision-making, while also understanding the economic principles at play. As such, they will be less likely to anchor to the first piece of information they receive because they will draw on their diverse knowledge to approach the situation with a willingness to be curious.

The Misinformation Effect

The misinformation effect is the tendency for memories to be heavily influenced by things that happened after the actual event. Even subtle influences such as questions or media coverage can alter our recollections, with consequences ranging from the trivial to the serious, as in the case of eyewitness testimony in criminal cases.

Here's a rather freaky example: At a family gathering, Mark shared a childhood story about getting lost in a theme park and being found by a clown who then returned him to his parents.

A few months later, his cousin, who heard the story, tells it to others but adds that Mark was so scared of the clown that he cried. The next time Mark recounts the story, he includes the detail about crying, even though he hadn't been afraid and hadn't cried in the original incident. The misinformation becomes real to Mark and alters his memory.

A multidisciplinary background can help us recognize and filter out misleading information. For example, someone with a background in psychology, neuroscience, and statistics would be better equipped to critically evaluate studies that claim to have found evidence of the misinformation effect; again, insatiable curiosity is at play.

In addition, a multidisciplinary background can enhance our communication skills, making us better at explaining complex concepts and identifying areas where information may be unclear or ambiguous, helping to reduce the likelihood of misinformation being spread and enabling us to make more informed decisions based on accurate information.

To Thine Own Self Be True

We take some shortcuts to claim our successes and mask our failures. When we excel, we often credit our own skills and hard work, but when we fall short we tend to attribute it to factors like misfortune, uncontrollable situations, or the deeds of others. This inclination aids in safeguarding our self-worth, yet it can also result in inaccurate conclusions, overconfidence, and a failure to take responsibility, hindering us from gleaning insights from our errors.

It's interesting to note that age and gender can also play a role in the self-serving bias. Older people are more likely to take credit for their successes, while men are more likely to blame outside forces for their failures.

I'm see this bias in the courtroom all the time. When a lawyer won a jury trial, they walked away with bravado, as if they were the champion of the universe, but, when they lost, they blamed the judge or the jury. Certainly, it wasn't something *they* did.

When we live in multiple lanes we experience more things that we wouldn't otherwise have, making us more likely to admit defeat and learn something new. This can help us overcome the self-serving bias by providing us with a broader perspective and a deeper understanding of the factors that contribute to success and failure.

For example, someone with a background in psychology may be more aware of the cognitive biases that can lead to overconfidence and may be more likely to recognize their own limitations. Someone with a background in economics may be more aware of the role that incentives and external factors can play in shaping outcomes and may be more likely to take these factors into account when evaluating their own performance.

Also, the more you embrace learning and taking on new challenges, the more failure becomes an everyday thing. The more you learn, the less afraid you are of failure. Thus, you see around the self-serving filter.

From My Perspective...

We tend to apply a different filter to ourselves than we do to others. There is a cognitive tendency to attribute our own actions to external influences and other people's actions to internal ones, leading to misunderstanding, miscommunication, and errors in judgment and decision-making. If you think of the example I just discussed about a lawyer blaming a judge and jury for their failure, it would be the same lawyer claiming his prowess after winning a trial, but easily assigning a poor assessment to a lawyer who lost the same case because he was "inefficient and a bad lawyer."

Overcoming this self-protection filter requires a multi-faceted approach. Cultivating self-awareness is crucial, and recognizing the bias is the first step in combating it. Empathy and perspective, combined with a reluctance to make rushed judgments, can help one better understand the external factors that influence others.

Seeking diverse experiences, especially those provided by a multidisciplinary background, can offer varied lenses through which one views situations, promoting a broader understanding of different perspectives. Additionally, mindfulness practices and processing feedback from trusted peers further fortify this endeavor. With the continuous learning that a multidisciplinary is used to you will acquire a more holistic view of yourself as well. You will not need to protect yourself nearly as much; you will be comfortable in your own skin.

The False Consensus Effect

In some situations, we tend to overestimate how much other people agree with our beliefs, behaviors, attitudes, and values. This shortcut is driven by the people we spend the most time with and our desire for self-esteem. It can lead to an overvaluation of our own opinions and a lack of consideration for the perspectives of others, also leading to misunderstandings, conflicts, and poor decision-making.

My wife comes from a family that has an extremely high tolerance for spicy food. They didn't think anything of putting hot sauce on everything. The first time my wife made a tossed salad with chopped jalapeños in it she brought me to my knees in pain. The look on her face was priceless. She had lived under the false consensus that everyone ate spicy food.

When we walk in different lanes, we see people thinking differently in every lane. This exposure to the thoughts and feelings of people in multiple lanes gives us a greater ability to find out what people think rather than jumping to conclusions. We recognize that not everyone sees the world the same way, and we can adjust our own beliefs and behaviors accordingly.

The more lanes we walk in the greater our ability to communicate more effectively with others who may have different perspectives. We can draw on our knowledge of different fields to find common ground and build consensus, rather than assuming that everyone shares our own beliefs and values.

The Halo Effect

The halo effect is a common cognitive shortcut. We tend to make generalizations about people based on our initial visual impression of them. For example, if we meet someone who is physically attractive, we may assume that they are also kind, intelligent, and funny, leading us to overlook other important qualities that may not be immediately apparent.

One interesting thing about the halo effect is that it can also influence how we perceive products or brands. If a product is marketed by an attractive person, we may assume that it is also of higher quality or value. This can have real-world implications, as companies use this bias to their advantage in their advertising campaigns.

Right now, you should automatically be thinking that multidisciplinarians look deeper. Ultimately, biases can be overcome by having the awareness to identify and challenge our own tendency to take a shortcut and be willing to jump to System 2 to think about the situation. For instance, if you are aware of your tendency to give undue weight to someone's positive qualities based on their overall impression of them, you can work to counteract this by intentionally looking at each trait or characteristic individually and assessing each on its own merit.

The Availability Heuristic

The availability heuristic makes us rely on the most recent or vivid examples that come to mind when we try to estimate the probability of something happening. It can lead to inaccurate assessments of risk and create unnecessary fears or a false sense of security. For instance, if you hear about several shark attacks on the news you might avoid going to the beach, even though the chances of being attacked by a shark are very low.

The availability heuristic is a shortcut we take to rely on easily available or accessible information in making judgments or decisions rather than seeking out and considering all relevant information. This is something Daniel Kahneman called WYSIATI, which means *What You See Is All There Is*. Bottom line, we take the shortcut by simply relying upon only the information that's in front of us so we unconsciously don't have to think about it anymore. It's just easier. The multidisciplinarian is less likely to rely on a narrow range of information and more likely to consider different angles and viewpoints.

If Jane worries about the effects of late-night eating, her confirmation bias is easily exacerbated by the fact that she may also be more influenced by the most recent or emotionally charged information she sees. That is a combination of biases, and it will cast a heavier shadow on the decision-making process.

The shortcut is easy to circumvent by simply pushing yourself intentionally into System 2 and thinking about the circumstances. This is a very common trick for those who are lifelong learners.

Looking Through Rose-Colored Glasses

It's funny, but sometimes multidisciplinarians are optimistic in their knowledge, yet they don't see the world through rose-colored glasses. They are too prone to question everything. When we're *absolutely optimistic* we believe that we're immune to negative events or that they're less likely to happen to us than to others. It can make us take risks or avoid necessary precautions, assuming that we won't be affected. For instance, some of us don't wear helmets when riding bikes because we believe accidents only happen to other people. This bias can lead us to overestimate our chances of success and underestimate our risk of failure, which can negatively impact our decision-making and planning.

When we have a broader understanding of different domains, we're less likely to be overly optimistic or overly pessimistic about a situation. We tend to be realistic.

Rather than jumping to conclusions, we would be more likely to explore all facets of a situation before concluding that it's a good or bad idea. That's what makes us more innovative. The multidisciplinary approach leads to a more balanced and informed attitude, reducing the likelihood of being overly optimistic or pessimistic.

That's the Way It's Always Been

Our decisions often come up against the status quo. There's a human tendency to prefer the current situation over any alternative, even if the alternative could be better. Looking back on the past and using it as a filter to view the future can get in the way of positive change or innovation. This bias is commonly phrased in the workplace as, *But that's the way we've always done it around here.*

Digging in and saying *That's the way we do it* means *I don't want to think about it*. Consider the fact that something new is a fantastic learning opportunity and should be explored. Digging in and maintaining the status quo is a shortcut that shuts down a lot of progress.

For example, if you're working in a company that's been using the same outdated software for years, you may suggest an alternative that can increase efficiency and productivity. Being open to change and willing to take risks can help you overcome the status quo bias.

Isn't That a Coincidence

By human nature we have a tendency to see patterns or connections in random and unrelated information. This is called *Apophenia*. This filter can lead us to draw conclusions that are not supported by evidence, which can lead to poor decision-making and incorrect conclusions.

In a business, apophenia might occur when a marketing team interprets random fluctuations in website traffic as meaningful patterns. For example, if a company's website experiences a sudden increase in visitors on a particular day, the marketing team might mistakenly attribute this to a recent change in their social media strategy, even if there's no direct evidence to support that connection. This tendency to perceive patterns or causality where none exists can lead to misguided decision-making, such as allocating more resources to an ineffective marketing campaign based on a perceived correlation that is actually coincidental.

To avoid apophenia, realize that pushing yourself to do some System 2 thinking will allow you to rely on data and empirical evidence rather than intuition or subjective judgments. Analyzing data can help us recognize real patterns and connections, which can lead to more accurate and informed decision-making.

Framing is a filter we construct to "frame" a problem so it can be more easily understood and presented, which can greatly affect the outcome. Later in this book, when we're discussing dealing with unknowns, we'll talk more about framing in the perspective of narratives.

Let's look again at the marketing team interpreting web traffic. Framing bias leads them to frame the situation in a positive light, attributing success to their actions when, in reality, the increase in traffic could be due to unrelated factors. The team overestimates the effectiveness of their strategy and makes decisions based on a skewed view of their achievements. Why? Again, we are pulled toward the easier conclusion rather than fully engaging our System 2 process.

To avoid framing bias, understand how a problem is presented and critically evaluate the information presented. Questions like, *What assumptions underlie this information?* and *What other interpretations are possible?* can help us consider alternative perspectives and make informed decisions.

Think More

Awareness of biases is crucial to making informed decisions. Status quo bias, apophenia, framing, and others can negatively affect our decision-making. Being open to change, relying on data and empirical evidence, and critically evaluating information, all aided and abetted by a multidisciplinary mindset, can overcome these biases and help us make informed decisions.

Venturing into the mind's labyrinth, we unearth the subtle biases that sculpt our perceptions and choices. It's as if our brains dance on strings, easily manipulated into weaving stories not always rooted in reality.

Confirmation bias lures us into self-affirming bubbles; or hindsight whispers that events were 'always in the cards;' or mesmerized by a person's charm we unwittingly overlook their flaws—a classic 'halo effect;' or perhaps our memories play tricks, making familiar events seem more probable due to the availability heuristic. All of these problems can be vanquished through greater awareness of our biases.

Don't Get Too Comfortable

At the core of our belief system is an intriguing phenomenon—*confidence by coherence*. Generally speaking, this theory means we feel more confident in our beliefs when they fit together nicely, even if the evidence isn't very strong.

The best way for me to describe this and prepare you to overcome it would be to put you in a specific situation from my life. I represented hundreds of criminal clients, but the worst were the ones who came to every meeting, every court hearing, and every interview with their mother.

In addition to a hodgepodge of all the biases we've discussed, moms paint a certain picture of their children. No matter how weak their knowledge is of current events, or how weak their evidence is to contradict the criminal charges, they have created a very tight little story that fits together so well in their minds that their confidence cannot be shaken. Nothing will convince them that their story is full of holes.

What makes people blind to the facts in such a situation is their deep love and belief in an individual. In their mind, they are extremely confident in their belief because their belief fits together coherently regardless of the strength of the underlying evidence or the validity of their story.

In short, when our beliefs align in a way to create a consistent narrative or worldview, we are more likely to feel confident in those beliefs. This can sometimes lead to overlooking contradictory evidence or not questioning weak evidence if it supports our coherent set of beliefs.

When someone approaches a situation holistically and can see everything, they are less inclined to write a narrative that doesn't fit the situation. Even the best specialist needs to be reminded not to develop a set of interconnected beliefs or models within their domain from which they cannot move. Doing so might subject them to an echo chamber response, confirmation bias, or even expertise-induced bias.

Don't Drink the Kool-Aid

In the grand game of decision-making, biases can sometimes trip us up like untied shoelaces. It's always wise to take a second look before jumping on a bandwagon or, say, drinking the Kool-Aid.

By keeping an eye out for those sneaky biases and tackling them head-on, we're on track for clearer thinking and better choices. That's the beauty of being a generalist. With knowledge spanning across various fields, you're less likely to get swept up by the latest hype or get stuck in a one-track mindset.

Thankfully, wearing a generalist's hat gives us a wider view, helping us place new tidbits of information in just the right spots. It's the obsession with lifelong learning that the cross-disciplinary thinker unleashes on all they do. We want to know more; we embrace our ignorance and seek more information before we make a decision.

The awesome part is that because we multidisciplinarians have a network of domains at our disposal, we make quick work of the decision process. It is—for us—not laborious at all. It's exciting! *We are a bit foxy that way.*

JOURNEY MILEPOSTS

- **The Power of Multidisciplinary Knowledge in Decision-Making:** In this chapter, the transformative impact of having a multidisciplinary background on decision-making is discussed. As you absorb the insights, consider how nurturing skills and knowledge across various fields enriches your perspective, allowing for a more nuanced and multifaceted approach to making decisions. How has your existing repertoire of multidisciplinary skills influenced the way you perceive and resolve challenges? Engage in a reflective exploration of instances where a varied skill set has enhanced your decision-making process, enabling a broader and more enlightened viewpoint, unconstrained by the tunnel vision of specialization.

- **Navigating Cognitive Biases through a Multidisciplinary Lens:** There's a significant emphasis on recognizing and mitigating cognitive biases, a challenge intricately woven into the fabric of human decision-making. Contemplate how a multidisciplinary background acts as a catalyst in unveiling and overcoming these inherent biases. How does exposure to diverse fields and methodologies arm you with the tools to effectively navigate the labyrinth of cognitive biases? Invigorate your thought process by evaluating how a varied knowledge base can be a powerful ally in dismantling biases, promoting a decision-making approach that is both balanced and enlightened by a spectrum of perspectives.

- **Self-Awareness and Growth:** Many of these biases, such as the self-serving bias and the halo effect, touch on the theme of self-awareness. Reflect on moments when you may have fallen prey to these biases. How do they serve or hinder your personal growth? How might acknowledging and confronting these biases lead to more fulfilling relationships, professional advancements, and personal insights?

- **Societal Implications:** Biases don't just operate on an individual level; they permeate group dynamics, institutional structures, and societal norms. How do you think these biases might influence larger societal decisions, from political elections to the marketing strategies of global brands? How might we, as a society, create checks and balances to ensure these biases don't lead to misleading narratives or unjust practices?

- **Reflect** on a time in your life when you confidently believed in something that, upon further examination, was not strongly supported by evidence. How did the coherence of that belief shape your confidence in it? With the insights gained from this reading, how might you approach similar situations differently in the future, especially by leveraging a multidisciplinary mindset?

10

The Strategist: Seeing the Future

There are known knowns. There are things we know that we know. There are known unknowns. That is to say, there are things that we know we don't know. But there are also unknown unknowns. There are things we don't know we don't know.
— Donald Rumsfeld, former United States Secretary of Defense

When it comes to facing the challenges of a world of radical uncertainty, people with multidisciplinary backgrounds have a unique advantage. Our arsenal is stocked with diverse tools and an enriched mindset that empower us to sift through ambiguity, celebrate the nuances of diversity, and dissect challenges from multiple perspectives.

In this chapter, we will explore decision-making in an uncertain world. We'll discuss the value of a multidisciplinary mind and how it can be leveraged to create a more resilient and innovative response. Shedding light on the benefits of cross-disciplinary collaboration, we will grasp how it can lead to breakthroughs in science, technology, and the arts; a primer on how to develop the skills necessary to thrive in a world of radical uncertainty.

The Ubiquity of Uncertainty

Donald Rumsfeld's statement, above, might seem confusing, but what he was getting at was the idea that there are always going to be things we don't know. And, crucially, *we might not even know that we don't know them.*

This idea is particularly relevant in a world where we are faced with new and complex challenges every day. We might think we have all the information we need to make a decision, but there might be important pieces of information that we don't even know exist.

In recent times, one cannot help but think of one of the most jarring unknown unknowns that we faced in the current era: COVID-19. Governments worldwide grappled with unprecedented challenges, having to make critical choices with limited and rapidly evolving information. Without a contemporary blueprint to navigate such a vast global health crisis, leaders in government and business made swift decisions, sometimes based on incomplete data, reflecting the essence of operating under extreme unpredictability and uncertainty.

From the unpredicted twists in global events to the inexplicable intricacies of individual human behavior, uncertainty continues to challenge our assumptions, plans, and strategies. Yet it's this very uncertainty that drives innovation, resilience, and adaptability, compelling us to evolve, adapt, and find meaning in the midst of ambiguity. Embracing uncertainty, rather than fearing it, is the key to navigating the complexities of the modern world. But unknowns must be approached correctly if we seek positive results.

The concept of unknown unknowns is a reminder that we need to approach problems with a healthy dose of humility. We can't assume we know everything there is to know about a situation. We need to be open to new information and new perspectives, even if they challenge our preconceived notions.

This idea is especially important for leaders. When we're in positions of power it's easy to fall into the trap of thinking we have all the answers. But the truth is, we don't. We need to be open to feedback and criticism, and we need to be willing to change our minds if new information comes to light.

Radical Uncertainty

I would be remiss discussing radical uncertainty without commenting upon the financial crisis of 2007-2008 which stands as a stark testament to the concept of radical uncertainty.

For those of you who weren't here to live through it, simply imagine a situation in which, in a matter of several months, the US housing market collapsed, sparking a crash that caused stock markets to plummet and economies to enter recession. From my perspective, my real estate title agency went from a lucrative business to an eight-dollar bank account and tens of thousand dollars in payroll in a matter of a month and a half. It was swift.

While intricate financial models, deeply entrenched in their specific domains, projected an image of resilience and growth, they were blindsided by cascading events that shook the global economy. These models, with their narrowed focus, were unable to factor in the wider range of variables and interactions that could lead to such a downturn. That is why the downturn took the world quickly and suddenly.

It poses the question: Could a generalist—a fox—with a broader view of interconnected systems and a more holistic understanding of global dynamics, have foreseen the impending crisis? In the complex tapestry of the global economy, where finance, behavior, politics, and culture intertwine, perhaps a generalist's perspective could have provided the foresight that many specialized models lacked, illuminating the gaps and underscoring the value of broad-based perspectives.

Frankly, I would love to have had a generalist in my financial planner's corner.

Risk and Uncertainty

The term *radical uncertainty* was coined by Frank Knight, an American economist, in the early 20th century. Knight was interested in the concept of risk and uncertainty in economic decision-making. He argued that there were two types of uncertainty: *risk* and *uncertainty*.

Risk, he argued, is the type of uncertainty that can be measured and quantified. For example, if you were flipping a coin, you could calculate the probability of it landing on heads or tails. That's a risk.

Uncertainty, on the other hand, is the type of uncertainty that can't be measured or predicted. It's what Knight called radical uncertainty. It's the kind of uncertainty that we face in everyday life, where we can't predict outcomes with any precision. It's a type of uncertainty that is inherent in many of the decisions we make. It's the uncertainty that cannot be quantified or predicted by traditional models or methods and it's increasingly prevalent in today's world as we face complex challenges and rapid change.

Knight believed that radical uncertainty was an essential part of economic decision-making. In fact, he argued that it was what made entrepreneurship possible. Entrepreneurs take risks, but they also face radical uncertainty. They can't predict the future, but they take a leap of faith and hope for the best.

Why is this important? For starters, it means we need to be prepared for the unexpected. We can't rely on our usual methods of forecasting or risk analysis. We need to be ready to adapt to changing circumstances and pivot quickly when necessary.

But radical uncertainty isn't just about being prepared for the worst. It's also about embracing the potential for new and unexpected opportunities. When we acknowledge that we don't know everything we open ourselves up to new discoveries and innovations.

Decision-making is an integral part of our lives. We make decisions every day, from what to eat for breakfast to what career to pursue. In some cases, we may have all the information we need to make an informed decision. However, there are situations where we face radical uncertainty, where we cannot predict the future with any degree of certainty due to incomplete or insufficient information. In such situations, relying on traditional decision-making models and probabilistic approaches may not be adequate.

This is where the ideas of John Kay and Mervyn King come into play. In their book *Radical Uncertainty: Decision-Making Beyond the Numbers,* Kay and King argue that radical uncertainty is an inevitable part of decision making, and we must find other ways to make good decisions when traditional approaches aren't effective.

The concept of radical uncertainty challenges us to think differently about the world around us. It encourages us to be humble in the face of the unknown and to embrace uncertainty as a natural part of life. It also encourages us to minimize unknowns to the greatest extent we can. How do we do that?

Knowing the Unknowns

To resolve radical uncertainty, King and Kay suggest that we should embrace the idea of *unknowability* and develop heuristics or rules of thumb that allow us to make reasonable decisions based on the limited information available. These heuristics should be flexible and adaptable to changing circumstances, and they should also be informed by feedback and learning from past decisions.

Another way to resolve radical uncertainty is through scenario planning, which involves developing and evaluating multiple plausible scenarios based on different assumptions about the future. This can help us anticipate and prepare for different outcomes and make more informed decisions.

King and Kay also recommend building resilience by maintaining a diversity of options and avoiding over-commitment to any particular course of action. This can help individuals navigate through uncertain and unpredictable environments and respond to unexpected changes or events. By embracing unknowability, using heuristics, scenario planning, and building resilience, we can make better decisions and respond to changing circumstances in uncertain environments.

Interestingly, Kay and King also suggest that specialists, people with a narrow focus and deep knowledge in a specific field, may be at a disadvantage when it comes to decision making under radical uncertainty. They argue that generalists, people with a broad range of knowledge and experiences, may have an advantage in these situations because generalists can draw from a variety of fields and perspectives, allowing them to develop more diverse and robust heuristics for decision making.

King and Kay argue that specialists may be more prone to overconfidence or tunnel vision, which can lead to suboptimal decisions. They suggest that decision-making under radical uncertainty requires a multidisciplinary approach, where individuals with diverse backgrounds and expertise can collaborate to develop heuristics that are more accurate and effective. The narrow view of a single expert can lead decision-makers to overestimate the reliability of their predictions, which can be misleading and result in poor decisions. Instead, when facing radical uncertainty, decision-makers need to adopt a more holistic and diverse approach to decision-making that includes multiple perspectives, sources of data, and methods of analysis. King and Kay's view of specialists in decision-making is that they may not necessarily have an advantage over non-specialists, and that a multidisciplinary approach may be more effective. By focusing on heuristics and collaborating with individuals with diverse backgrounds and expertise, decision-makers can make more informed choices, even under conditions of high uncertainty.

One way to do this is through scenario planning, which involves considering multiple plausible scenarios for the future and developing strategies that are robust across a range of outcomes. Another approach is to use probabilistic forecasting, which involves quantifying uncertainties and considering the range of possible outcomes and their probabilities. The future is inherently uncertain, and predicting what will happen is challenging.

Two Potential Solutions: Narratives and Nudging

Narratives refer to the stories we tell ourselves about the future. In situations of radical uncertainty, narratives can help provide a framework for decision-making. By creating a plausible and internally consistent story about the future, we can create a mental model that allows us to better understand risks and opportunities, helping us make more informed decisions, even in the face of significant uncertainty.

Nudging, on the other hand, refers to the idea of using subtle cues or incentives to influence decision-making. In situations of radical uncertainty, nudging is particularly effective because it can help to guide decision-making without requiring a complete understanding of the future. By presenting options in a way that encourages certain behaviors, nudging can help steer decision-making towards more desirable outcomes.

Imagine that a company is considering whether to invest in a new product line. In a situation of radical uncertainty, it may be difficult to predict how the market will respond to the new product. In this situation, a narrative approach could involve creating a compelling story about how the new product fits into the company's overall strategy and how it is likely to perform in the market. This could help the decision-makers feel more confident in their decision.

A nudging approach, on the other hand, could involve presenting the decision-makers with a series of options that are designed to encourage investment in the new product line. This might involve presenting data about the potential returns on investment or highlighting the success of similar products.

Both narratives and nudging are effective tools for decision-making in situations of radical uncertainty. By providing a framework for decision-making and guiding decision-makers towards more desirable outcomes, they can help reduce the risks associated with uncertain situations.

Here's another example of nudging: placing healthier food options at eye level in a grocery store, with less-healthy options placed higher or lower on the shelves, makes it easier for people to choose healthier options without necessarily limiting their choices. Another example is having default options on a website or app. For instance, when setting up a new email account, the default option might be to sign up for promotional emails, which people can opt out of if they wish.

While nudging can be a useful tool in decision-making, some critics argue that it can feel manipulative, and that it assumes that the person doing the nudging knows what's best for others. Others argue that nudging is only effective for simple or straightforward decisions, and that more complex choices require more direct methods of influence. Nudging is an interesting concept that raises questions about how we make decisions and the role that external factors can play in our choices.

Kay and King argue that nudging can be a useful tool for decision-making under radical uncertainty because it can help individuals make better decisions without necessarily requiring them to have complete information or to be able to predict the future. By designing the choice environment in a way that encourages certain behaviors or decisions, nudges can help individuals make better decisions that align with their interests, values, and goals.

On the other hand, Cass Sunstein and Richard Thaler, proponents of the nudge theory, believe that nudging can help individuals make better decisions without restricting their freedom of choice[1]. They define a nudge as any aspect of the choice architecture that alters people's behavior in a predictable way without forbidding any options or significantly changing economic incentives. They suggest that nudging can be used to guide individuals towards decisions that are in their best interest without resorting to coercion.

Sunstein and Thaler suggest that nudges should be designed to be subtle, easy, and inexpensive to implement. They also emphasize the importance of transparency and ethical considerations. Nudges should be designed to benefit the individual or society as a whole, and not just to serve the interests of those implementing the nudges. Additionally, individuals should be made aware of the nudges being used and have the freedom to opt out or make a different decision.

When it comes to resisting nudging in decision-making, generalists are less likely to be nudged. Their broad range of knowledge and experience makes them resistant to the influence of a single perspective or way of thinking. They're able to take a more holistic approach to decision-making and consider multiple factors and perspectives before making a choice. People with multidisciplinary backgrounds are uniquely equipped to navigate the complexities of decision-making under radical uncertainty, and they instinctively understand

---

[1] Thaler, Richard H., and Cass R. Sunstein. Nudge: Improving Decisions about Health, Wealth, and Happiness. Penguin Books, 2009.

how their skills can be leveraged to respond to challenges and chart a course towards a more sustainable, equitable, and resilient future. Specifically, we will examine how the ability to deconstruct narratives and understand the ways in which they influence decision-making, as well as the role of nudges in shaping behavior, is bolstered by a multidisciplinary perspective.

More about Narratives

Narratives serve as useful and indispensable tools when it comes to making decisions in a state of extreme uncertainty. Kay and King contend that these stories provide essential roles to our decision-making processes.

Rather than viewing narratives as deceptive, they are actually an invaluable means of arriving at judgments when probabilistic conclusions are difficult to come by. To this end, they aid us in making sense of an abstract concept, as metaphors, analogies, and other forms of linguistics serve to give it more of a tangible form. These elements help us answer the question, "What is happening?" Even if mathematical or quantitative data are present, narratives can help make sense of the facts.

A single narrative cannot be applicable to every complex circumstance. As new information is absorbed, our reference stories must be subject to constant adjustment. Many people prefer a broad and sweeping grand narrative that can be implemented in a wide range of settings, but given the flux and complexity of radical uncertainty, grand narratives are rarely realistic. And narratives are not solely confined to stories, as they encompass models and other conceptual apparatuses to illustrate a theoretical situation in which certain characters behave in certain ways.

To make a narrative effective, it needs to be believable and consistent with both the internal details and the external information. Despite this, a narrative doesn't have to be factual; a hypothetical tale can still yield the appropriate reference data to navigate through uncertainty. Additionally, it should be noted that narratives have tangible effects on the real world: Economists employ miniature models to illustrate grandiose concepts, which are, themselves, narratives.

Rather than judging the narratives based on whether they are true or false, it's more beneficial to determine whether or not they're practical. If they aren't, they must be altered accordingly. This underscores the scientific way of thinking—an inclination to be receptive to new knowledge and accept that modifications to the narrative may be required.

The City of Gold

Narratives and nudging have immense power to influence our perceptions and decisions, often guiding society's course.

Historically, the allure of the 'City of Gold' sent explorers into the unknown, and although they never found El Dorado, nor did they find the gold they sought, the narrative itself inspired their journeys that led to monumental discoveries. Similarly, today's 'Silicon Valley innovation' narrative magnetizes global talent and capital, orchestrating the pace of technological progress. Yet with the power of these narratives comes an ethical responsibility: ensuring they don't mislead or harm.

Concurrently, nudging—a subtler form of influence—can be observed in varied sectors. Whether it's graphic cigarette warnings aiming to deter smokers or recycling initiatives designed to promote eco-friendly habits, the intention is to subtly steer behaviors. In finance, the automatic enrollment of employees into retirement plans capitalizes on inertia, while online platforms employ tactics like 'infinite scroll' to boost user engagement.

As influential as they are, narratives and nudging techniques both pose ethical questions: At what point does influence become manipulation? It's essential to strike a balance between guidance and autonomy, ensuring that individuals aren't unduly swayed or misled.

Looking at the above risks and issues from a general viewpoint, it's important to point out that our contemporary challenges, whether in economics, technology, or social spheres, are seldom isolated. Today's challenges stem from intersections of various disciplines from history to biology.

The narrative of the City of Gold isn't just about exploration but about human aspiration, ambition, and the shared mission to propel society forward. Similarly, the concept of nudging isn't just a behavioral economic tool. It also taps into deep rooted biological instinct and learned social behaviors. Looking at such things from a generalist approach highlights the importance of this integrated knowledge, deepens understanding of its interconnectedness, and fosters a holistic perspective.

The Medium Is the Message

The way a message is conveyed is extraordinarily important. It's how one creates understanding. Remember Marshall McLuhan from an earlier chapter? His concept of the *medium is the message* suggests that the medium through which information is conveyed is just as important as the information itself. In other words, the way information is presented can impact the way it is received and understood. McLuhan's work on the impact of technology on human consciousness can help individuals who are proficient in multiple disciplines understand how technology and communication impact their decision-making processes. McLuhan believed that technology had a profound impact on the way people thought and communicated with each other. For individuals who are proficient in multiple disciplines, this impact can be particularly significant because they are likely to encounter a wide range of technological tools and communication methods in their work.

For example, someone who is proficient in both finance and information technology might be involved in a decision about implementing a new financial software system. The decision-making process will likely involve a range of communication methods, including email, video conferencing, and face-to-face meetings. McLuhan's work suggests that the medium through which these communication methods occur can impact the decision-making process. Additionally, McLuhan's work on the concept of *the global village* highlights the interconnectedness of the modern world and the impact of decisions made in one part of the world on people and cultures in another. This concept is particularly relevant for individuals who are proficient in multiple disciplines because they are likely to encounter a wide range of perspectives and cultural norms in their work.

McLuhan's concept of *the medium is the message* and his concept of *the global village* highlight the importance of understanding how different mediums, communication methods, and cultural perspectives impact the decision-making process. By incorporating these insights into their decision-making processes, individuals who are proficient in multiple disciplines can make better informed decisions and achieve better outcomes.

This concept is particularly relevant for individuals who are proficient in multiple disciplines because they are likely to encounter a variety of mediums and methods for receiving information. Someone who can distill all their diverse skills into a single narrative can create a message that is much stronger than that which would be created by a specialist. There is more raw material to draw from in a more diverse mind.

When it comes to innovating and making decisions, the ability to build compelling narratives is essential. People react very differently depending upon how messages are delivered. A well-crafted story has the power to inspire, engage, and connect with others, and those with a multidisciplinary mindset are particularly adept at this. By drawing on different disciplines and experiences, they can create narratives that not only address the problem at hand but also consider broader implications.

In addition to their narrative-building skills, individuals with a multidisciplinary mindset are also more likely to challenge assumptions and take calculated risks. They are comfortable with ambiguity and can navigate complex problems, often finding creative solutions that others may overlook.

People with a wider breadth of experience and knowledge are better at building narratives as a means of innovating and making decisions because they bring unique perspectives to the table. They combine different disciplines and experiences to create compelling stories that inspire and motivate others. The use of narratives in decision-making requires an understanding of linguistics, cognitive psychology, and economics, among other fields. Multidisciplinary individuals may be able to draw upon these and other fields to create narratives that are both credible and coherent, and that can be revised as new information becomes available. They are also able to recognize that different narratives may be more useful in different contexts, and that flexibility and openness to adjustment are essential components of effective decision-making.

The Rumsfeld Corollary: We Don't Know Everything

When making decisions, we often rely on information and past experiences to predict what will happen in the future. Probabilistic approaches are methods that use statistical models and historical data to predict outcomes. However, there are some situations where these methods may not be effective, and this is where radical uncertainty comes into play.

It's difficult to predict the future with a high degree of certainty when there's incomplete or insufficient information. In these situations, probabilistic approaches may not be adequate to guide decision-making. This means that we cannot rely on past experiences or statistical models to make decisions, and we must find other ways to make good choices. In this context, the *Bayesian* dial refers to the degree to which a Bayesian model is used to estimate uncertainty. Bayesian models, you'll recall from earlier in the book, are a type of probabilistic model that incorporates prior beliefs about the world to update estimates of uncertainty as new data becomes available.

Radical uncertainty theorists argue that the Bayesian dial may not be appropriate for dealing with deep uncertainty, because Bayesian models rely on the assumption that all uncertainty can be modeled as a probability distribution. However, radical uncertainty suggests that there may be important sources of uncertainty that are difficult or impossible to quantify in this way.

Generalists are at an advantage here because Bayes's theorem can be applied to a wide variety of problems across many different fields. Generalists, who have a broad range of knowledge across different domains, are better equipped to recognize when and where Bayes's theorem might be useful.

For example, Bayes's theorem can be used to:

- predict the likelihood of a particular medical diagnosis based on a patient's symptoms.

- determine the probability that a particular email is spam based on the words in the message.
- estimate the probability of a certain stock price given past market trends.
- assess the accuracy of a machine-learning algorithm by comparing its predicted probabilities with observed outcomes.

Each of these examples involves different domains of knowledge, from medicine to computer science to finance. A generalist who is familiar with these domains is better equipped to recognize the applicability of Bayes's theorem and to apply it effectively.

When it comes to leadership and being part of the decision-making process combining the use of narratives and nudges, individuals with skills in multiple disciplines can make better decisions.

Imagine a business owner who is trying to decide whether to expand their operations or invest in a new product line. By constructing narratives that incorporate input from stakeholders, including customers, employees, and investors, the business owner can gain a more comprehensive understanding of the potential benefits and drawbacks of each option. They can then use nudges, such as setting default parameters for the decision-making process, to help guide them towards the best decision.

Think of all this from the cunning perspective of the fox, as depicted in Isaiah Berlin's writings, and through the lens of a holistic, multidisciplinary thinker. Embracing the diversity of perspectives and insights from various sources and domains will help you better appreciate the intricate web of understanding. Just as the fox values the multiplicity of approaches to life, the multidisciplinary thinker recognizes that each strand of knowledge contributes to the rich complexity of our life experiences.

The world needs individuals who can think critically, adapt to new situations, and make decisions in the face of uncertainty. The multidisciplinarian functions as a living network of experiences and possesses the capability to assimilate their knowledge seamlessly into the unfamiliar, uncovering a sense of familiarity within the unknown.

JOURNEY MILEPOSTS

- **The Power and Responsibility of Narratives:** Narratives, whether about the City of Gold or the innovation-driven Silicon Valley, serve as significant drivers for human aspiration and action. They encapsulate not just stories but the essence of human ambition. How can we ensure that the narratives we embrace or propagate strike a balance between inspiration and ethical responsibility? Furthermore, in your own life, which narratives have influenced your decisions, aspirations, or beliefs, and how might they need refinement or reconsideration?

- **Mediums, Messages, and Multidisciplinary Insights:** Marshall McLuhan's The medium is the message emphasizes the importance of how information is conveyed. As you reflect on your experiences, how have different mediums shaped or altered your perception of messages? Additionally, given the potential advantages of a multidisciplinary mindset in creating compelling narratives, consider how combining diverse skills can not only enhance communication but also foster innovation. What are some ways in which you might integrate a multidisciplinary approach in your personal or professional endeavors?

- **Navigating Uncertainty:** Our rapidly changing world often presents situations of radical uncertainty where traditional probabilistic approaches may fall short. As you think about the decisions you make daily, how often do you find yourself operating under conditions of uncertainty? How can tools like narratives and Bayes's theorem be applied more broadly in such scenarios? Moreover, how might embracing a generalist perspective better equip you to navigate the complexities and uncertainties of modern life?

- **The Power of Multidisciplinary Thinking:** Reflect on the idea that individuals with diverse academic and experiential backgrounds possess a wider array of tools to address unknowns. How might a society that embraces and nurtures multidisciplinary education and collaboration be better poised to respond to unforeseen challenges, such as global pandemics or financial crises?

- **Navigating Radical Uncertainty:** As you've read, there are various strategies to manage the unpredictable, from heuristics to scenario planning. But how might you apply these principles in your own decision-making processes, both professionally and personally? Additionally, consider the potential pitfalls of relying too heavily on any single approach and the balance one must strike between flexibility and over-preparation.

- **Ethical Implications of Nudging:** While nudging can guide individuals towards beneficial decisions, it also walks a fine line between influence and manipulation. As you contemplate the use of narratives and nudges, ponder their ethical boundaries. How can we ensure that nudges maintain individual autonomy and are used for the greater good, rather than self-serving interests?

LEARN MORE

11

Learning Mindset: One Superpower at a Time

> *Live as if you were to die tomorrow. Learn as if you were to live forever.*
> — Mahatma Gandhi

Imagine if being a jack-of-all-trades could be your superpower. But what if trying to do everything at once is actually holding you back? Let's consider the magic of multidisciplinary learning and the importance of homing in on one thing at a time in our ever-distracting world.

If you are already multidisciplinary, now is the time to expand your reach. If you're ready to explore new lanes, you're about to enter an exciting time of your life. You're about to learn new things! Welcome to a fuller and happier life. But it doesn't come instantaneously. You're going to have to work for it. Yes, it's going to take a little effort on your part, but it will enable you to do so much more, and the more you learn the easier it becomes.

Once you embark on a learning process, you'll discover a myriad of benefits that will change how you live and work. As we've discussed throughout this book, it creates great personal growth because it will walk you through experiences, methodologies, and techniques that will change the way you think. As you explore new disciplines and acquire new information, your critical thinking and analytical skills will improve, allowing you to enhance your ability to retain information, and more importantly, increasing your ability to *process* information. Each discipline you learn will start to cross lanes with other disciplines. Even if you're studying art, you'll discover that a background in science and math is beneficial.

As you schedule time for learning, you'll take the initiative to structure your own learning process, establishing a routine, balancing multiple commitments, and effectively allocating your time. Mastering these skills will lead to greater productivity and achievement.

The Art of Learning

Before you can paint you have to mix colors on a palette. If you want a mauve hue, you must be able to determine proportions and blend pigments, understanding that you need 50% blue, 25% white, and 25% red. You might discover that by painting and following what is called *the rule of thirds*—focal points throughout the painting at 1/3 from the top, or 1/3 from the bottom, or 1/3 from the sides—can produce a more interesting and attractive composition. Even an artist needs to understand grade-school math.

Everything you know and learn becomes a foundation for everything else.

With your increased analytical skills, you'll start to see the benefits to the areas we've discussed throughout this book, such as problem-solving, communication, and innovation. The learning process itself is a discipline that's well worth mastering. Lifelong learners continually seek knowledge, set goals, and experience personal growth. You will develop the mindset of a multidisciplinary thinker simply by mastering the learning process.

As we dive into the concept of planning and learning, I'd like to address a personal pet peeve: *multitasking*. Your brain will think in multiple lanes all by itself; it's up to you to make it focus on one thing at a time.

Doing several tasks at once divides your attention and focus, leading to a decrease in overall production because your brain is constantly switching between tasks. You'll lose time. You'll lose focus. Being multidisciplinary and living in multiple lanes doesn't mean you have to simultaneously *act* in multiple lanes.

Brian May, the lead guitarist for Queen, is one of the world's top players. He is also a doctor of astrophysics. When you see him on stage, he's playing guitar, not writing a dissertation on astrophysics. He doesn't wear both hats at the same time. But the cool part is that if his two worlds do come together, he's ready to jump between lanes.

Focus on what you're learning. Do one thing at a time and you'll be better for the experience. It's about mindfulness.

Zen Focus

In his 1959 classic *Zen and Japanese Culture*, D.T. Suzuki discussed the spiritual and cultural aspects of the tea ceremony, or chado. He emphasized that the tea ceremony is not just about the act of making and drinking tea. Rather, it's a ritual that incorporates mindfulness, aesthetics, and a deep appreciation of the present moment. The tea ceremony is an opportunity to cultivate humility, attentiveness, and harmony with nature and others.

In his teachings and writings, Thích Nhất Hạnh, a Vietnamese Zen Buddhist monk, teacher, and poet, emphasized the importance of performing daily tasks, such as washing dishes, with complete mindfulness and presence. He suggested that, instead of viewing these tasks as chores, one should approach them as opportunities for meditation and reflection. By focusing on the task at hand, and being fully present while doing it, we can develop greater awareness. The idea is to treat seemingly mundane tasks as meditation, as opportunities to practice mindfulness and develop a sense of inner peace.

The art of washing dishes is a metaphor for absolute focus. When you wash the dishes, wash the dishes. Do nothing else. Pay attention to the feeling of the water, the texture of the dishes, the sound of flowing liquid, and the sight of the bubbles. Engage all your senses and be fully present in the moment. Perform each action deliberately and mindfully, from picking up a dish to scrubbing it and rinsing it off. Notice the movement of your hands, the movements of your muscles, and the rhythm of your actions.

When you wash the dishes, you're not just cleaning—you're practicing the art of mindfulness, learning how to bring that same dedicated concentration to everything else you do. Any multitasking is an interference. So, to be mindful as we learn, let's consider what washing the dishes *means*.

As you wash the dishes, be aware of your breath. Focus on the inhalations and exhalations, maintaining a steady and calm rhythm. This practice will help you stay centered and present during the task. Your mind might wander to various thoughts, emotions, or worries. Gently acknowledge those distractions and then return your focus to the sensations and actions of washing the dishes. This practice helps train the mind to stay focused and present in the moment. Recognize that each dish washed is a moment in time that will pass, and that life is a series of such moments. Embracing the impermanence of the present moment can foster a sense of gratitude, humility, and connection with the world around you.

In today's busy world, multitasking has become a way of life. We often find ourselves juggling multiple tasks, thinking it makes us more productive, when it's the fully holistic and immersive experience that creates a power learner and will allow you to be more productive, more driven, and more focused on everything you do.

If we're working on a project while also answering emails and responding to text messages, our brains are constantly shifting between different modes of thinking, making it difficult to stay focused. David E. Meyer, Jeffrey E. Evans, and Joshua S. Rubinstein conducted a study called "Executive Control of

Cognitive Processes in Task Switching," published in *The Journal of Experimental Psychology: Human Perception and Performance* in 2001. They found that there's a "switching cost" involved when we juggle multiple tasks and that multitasking can reduce productivity by as much as 40%, a casualty of the time and mental effort it takes to shift our focus from one task to another. It can even lead to a higher likelihood of making errors.

For example, imagine you're trying to write an important email while also answering the phone and checking social media. Your brain is constantly switching between tasks, which makes it difficult to focus on the email and ensure you're communicating clearly and accurately. You might miss important details, forget to attach a file, or make typos that could change the meaning of your message.

When we try to do several things at once it's easy to become confused or make mistakes, especially if the tasks require a high level of attention to detail. This can be especially true if we're trying to complete multiple complex tasks simultaneously.

Think about your own life. Multitasking can be mentally taxing, can cause you to feel stressed and overwhelmed, and can ultimately hurt your ability to focus, concentrate, and complete tasks efficiently. You'll experience far more peace and balance in your life if you compartmentalize your thinking and do one thing at a time. Stop dividing your attention and stressing yourself out.

To avoid multitasking, simply minimize distractions. That might mean putting your phone on do not disturb or, better yet, leaving it in another room. I am as guilty as anyone of constantly checking my phone and interrupting myself. But I am also very aware of the toll that it takes on my progress and clarity of thinking.

A 2008 research article entitled "The Cost of Interrupted Work: More Speed and Stress,[1]" examines the impact of interruptions on task performance, time management, and stress levels. The authors found that frequent interruptions led to increased stress, higher frustration levels, and a greater sense of time pressure. When people were interrupted, they tended to work faster to compensate for the lost time, but this often resulted in decreased accuracy and higher stress levels.

Stop causing yourself stress. You will find that you'll have much less mental fatigue if you focus on one task at a time. When you're washing the dishes wash the dishes. When you think about other things you aren't focusing on the dishes. Your distractions will result in you not doing a job that should have been easy or done well. You'll find yourself working harder to clean up your mistakes.

Prioritize your learning tasks and focus on one thing at a time. Give each task your full attention and ensure that you do it to the best of your ability. If you have multiple tasks to complete, break them into smaller, more manageable bits and tackle them one at a time.

I confess that multitasking appears to be a better way to get things done because we're making all this stuff happen at once.

---

[1] Mark, G., Gudith, D., & Klocke, U. (2008). The cost of interrupted work: more speed and stress. Proceedings of the SIGCHI Conference on Human Factors in Computing Systems, 107-110.

But if you take into account all of the errors, the anxiety level, and the stress, you'll see that multitasking creates a negative impact on your health and well-being far beyond the damage you do to the immediate project.

The idea of getting more done in less time seems appealing, but it's the number-one cause of burnout. There's just too much going on. Stop it.

The art of single tasking is a revolutionary act.

By embracing the principles of mindfulness and the lessons of undivided focus, we not only enhance our productivity but also enrich our experiences. Each moment, whether we're strategizing in a boardroom or simply washing dishes, offers an opportunity to be fully present.

As we cultivate this discipline of true engagement, we unlock a true connection to our tasks, our surroundings and, ultimately, to ourselves. Remember, it's not about juggling multiple tasks; it's about immersing yourself fully in each moment you spend on a task.

This is the heart of living a purposeful, impactful life.

JOURNEY MILEPOSTS

- **The Multidisciplinary Mindset:** Reflect on the balance between being a Jack-of-all-trades and honing a specific skill. How can one leverage multidisciplinary learning without becoming overwhelmed by trying to do everything at once? How have your own varied learnings enhanced your abilities in seemingly unrelated areas?

- **The True Nature of Productivity:** Consider the seductive allure of multitasking versus the depth achieved through singular focus. Can we redefine productivity not as doing more things at once but as fully engaging in one task at a time? How might our daily lives and overall well-being change if we prioritize depth over breadth?

- **The Ritual of Mindfulness in Everyday Tasks:** Drawing from the practice of washing dishes as a meditation, how might you transform other "mundane" daily tasks into moments of mindfulness? What tasks in your life can serve as opportunities for personal growth and grounding?

- **Impact of Constant Distractions:** Reflect on the "switching costs" and potential detrimental effects of

> multitasking. In your own life, where do you recognize these switching costs, and how might you take steps to minimize or eliminate them to achieve greater clarity and productivity?

12

The Books You Read: Beyond Boundaries

You will be the same person in five years as you are today except for the people you meet and the books you read.
— Charlie "Tremendous" Jones

The necessity of becoming multidisciplinary cannot be overstated. Neither can I overstate the need to be a voracious learner and reader as an essential tool in this pursuit. Developing a diverse reading list helps enable you to cultivate a multidisciplinary mindset and become a well-rounded thinker. Reading widely across various disciplines equips you with a broader knowledge base and a wider range of perspectives.

Explore your interests by deliberately selecting books, articles, and other sources from various disciplines, such as science, history, philosophy, art, and literature. Whenever possible, read primary sources to gain a deeper understanding. This allows you to engage directly with the thoughts and ideas of experts and pioneers, enhancing your comprehension of complex concepts.

When do you read? Make it a habit. Set aside dedicated time each day for reading. Like anything else, consistency is key. And when you're done reading, don't just close the book. Reflect on what you read. Ask yourself what you read, but more importantly, consider what you thought while you were reading it. This process of reflection enables you to identify patterns and relationships across disciplines, fostering a more multidisciplinary mindset. It involves asking questions about the content and considering the thoughts that were generated while reading. By reflecting on the material, individuals can deepen their understanding, identify biases, and recognize the implications of the ideas they encounter.

As an aside, there are mileposts at the end of each of my chapters. Asking yourself these kinds of questions when you read any book is how you retain, process, and grow. I believe in it so much that I made it easier for you in my book, but you should create your own questions when you read the books of others.

Reflection helps us integrate new information into existing knowledge, allowing us to see the bigger picture and make connections. Through this process, we can develop a more nuanced and comprehensive perspective on various subjects, ultimately becoming more effective problem-solvers and collaborators. By engaging in reading and reflection, we can foster a more comprehensive understanding of the world, enabling us to contribute meaningfully to the diverse challenges and opportunities that lie ahead.

The Mighty Amazon

Multidisciplinary learning is exemplified by the journey of Jeff Bezos, the founder of Amazon.com, who started with a modest online bookstore and went on to revolutionize multiple industries. One of the key factors behind his success is a multidisciplinary approach to problem-solving which allowed him to tackle the challenge of selling books online, a market that had previously been dominated by brick-and-mortar stores, and turn Amazon into the world's largest online retailer.

When Bezos founded Amazon in 1994, he had no experience in the retail industry. However, he approached the problem of selling books online as a complex one that required a deep understanding of customer behavior, logistics, and marketing. Bezos recognized that he needed a multidisciplinary team to help him achieve his goals. He hired people with diverse backgrounds in computer science, engineering, logistics, marketing, and finance to help him build Amazon.

Bezos understood that to succeed in the retail industry, he needed to understand his customers. He believed that customer experience was the key to success, and he spent a lot of time studying customer behavior and preferences, and used this knowledge to build a user-friendly website that offered a wide selection of books at competitive prices. Bezos also introduced features such as customer reviews, personalized recommendations, and one-click ordering, making it easier for customers to find and purchase the books they wanted.

Logistics was another key area that Bezos focused on. He knew that efficient and cost-effective logistics would be essential to the success of Amazon, so he and his team developed a sophisticated system that enabled them to quickly process and ship orders to customers all over the world. This system used data analytics to optimize the placement of warehouses and distribution centers, as well as developing advanced algorithms to manage inventory and shipping.

Marketing was also critical to success. Bezos understood the importance of building a strong brand and creating a loyal customer base, so he invested heavily in advertising and promotions and focused on building partnerships with publishers and authors to offer exclusive content to his customers.

Bezos's multidisciplinary approach to problem-solving allowed him to build Amazon into a global behemoth, with a market capitalization of over $1.5 trillion as of 2021. His focus on customer experience, logistics, and marketing has made Amazon a household name and a dominant player in the online retail industry.

Bezos infused his multidisciplinary attitude into his leadership team at Amazon. The Amazon team facilitates cross-disciplinary training through its internal mobility and job rotation programs. These initiatives provide employees with opportunities to explore different roles within the organization, enabling them to broaden their skill sets and gain exposure to various aspects of the business. By working in diverse roles and departments, employees develop a more comprehensive understanding of the company's operations and build collaborative relationships with colleagues from different disciplines. By providing access to educational resources and supporting professional development, Amazon encourages employees to continually expand their expertise and develop a multidisciplinary mindset.

Amazon wasn't always a globe-straddling behemoth. It started as a tiny company run largely by one man. Jeff Bezos's journey from starting a modest online bookstore to building one of the world's most influential companies began with enriching his mind by studying every facet of the business he wished to build. It serves as a testament to the power of reading, reflection, and the multidisciplinary approach. It's not just about selling products; it's about logistics, customer behavior, technology, content creation, and much more.

By constantly seeking knowledge and making connections across disciplines, Bezos was able to identify unique opportunities and develop innovative solutions to complex problems. This comprehensive understanding of the world allowed him to revolutionize industries, create new markets, and contribute meaningfully to the global economy.

The more you read, the more you find new areas of interest. Every topic you learn about leads to ten more. Thus, reading books is a powerful tool for achieving a multidisciplinary mindset and continuous learning. Books provide us with a vast repository of knowledge, experiences, and perspectives from experts in various fields. Through reading and reflection, we gain insights into different ways of thinking, understanding complex concepts, and developing critical thinking skills.

As you read and learn, keep in mind that the boundaries between disciplines, thoughts, and ideas are porous, and that the real magic happens at their intersections. Not only does reading expand your vocabulary and improve your communication skills, it also enhances your ability to empathize with others. Developing a habit of reading allows you to continuously expand your knowledge, skills, and creativity. It doesn't just make you a multidisciplinarian, it empowers you to be a more well-rounded human.

JOURNEY MILEPOSTS

- **Embracing a Multidisciplinary Mindset in Today's World:** Reflect on your own experiences and endeavors. How often have you found yourself boxed within a single discipline or way of thinking? Given he successes of visionaries like Jeff Bezos, who employed a multidisciplinary approach, how might embracing multiple disciplines benefit your personal and professional growth? What steps can you take to broaden your perspective?

- **Beyond Reading: The Act of Reflection:** While many of us commit time to reading, fewer dedicate moments to reflect upon what we've absorbed. Consider your past reading habits: How often do you set aside time to ponder over what you've read? Do you find this reflection enriches your comprehension? Delve deeper into the importance of this process and its role in enhancing your multidisciplinary mindset.

- **Intersecting Boundaries: Where Magic Happens:** True innovation often occurs at the crossroads of multiple disciplines. Can you recall a situation or an innovation you've come across that exemplifies this? How can we actively ensure that we're not just learning within silos, but seeking the rich intersections of knowledge?

- **Reading: A Gateway to Empathy and Broader Horizons:** Beyond its cognitive benefits, reading allows us to step into the shoes of others, granting us a richer perspective on the world. Reflect on the books that have transformed your worldview or enhanced your empathy. How does this deeper understanding influence your daily interactions and decisions? As you embark on your reading journey, how will you ensure it remains a tool for personal growth, empathy, and societal advancement?

13

Lifelong Learner: New Skills Every Day!

> *The world has always belonged to the stronger and will belong to them for many years to come. People only respect those who make themselves respected. Whoever becomes a lamb will find a wolf to eat him.*
> — Vilfredo Pareto

As a trial lawyer, I always joked about the fact that I was a "Jack of all trades and a master at whatever I was just doing." This comment came about because of the way I had to learn things for each trial that I conducted. In criminal law, people would come into court and bring in experts in forensic pathology, DNA evidence, arson investigations, forensic toxicology, and a myriad of other areas of expertise.

We talked about some of this in the chapter about developing mindset, but I want to further discuss the application of learning in *addition* to having the correct mindset. As you read earlier, some of the people who testified in cases were doctors and scientists who were at the top of their field. For instance, in a DUI case, I once had a defense lawyer bring in a forensic toxicologist to talk about the effect of blood alcohol on the body. In an arson case, I had to teach myself everything there was to know about arson. It all came down to me, being able to confront, challenge, and mitigate the evidence presented by a professional arson investigator. Before the trial, I knew nothing about arson.

My job was simple. I had to challenge these experts in their fields of expertise and question, dispute, and undermine their opinions. To do this, I had to become an expert in whatever they knew. Whatever the reason they came into court, that was my discipline du jour. I had to change hats for every trial. That meant I had to become an expert at everything quickly and proficiently. In that arson case I had to be an instant expert. I went through a process of learning everything I needed to know to cross-examine the expert and have him admit his mistakes and errors. It was my job to be the expert's expert.

With that type of career, I became a lifelong learner. I had to develop systems of learning that would be tested against the best in the business. And every time I did it, I became more excited and more fulfilled.

Being a lifelong learner isn't just beneficial for personal growth and fulfillment. It also serves as a vital foundation for multidisciplinary expertise. The importance of lifelong learning lies in its ability to foster intellectual curiosity and adaptability.

As new technologies emerge and the global landscape shifts, the most successful individuals are those who can learn, unlearn, and relearn to stay ahead of the curve. By cultivating a growth mindset and a commitment to continuous learning, you can develop the resilience and agility necessary to navigate the challenges and uncertainties of the modern world.

Continuous learning also plays a crucial role in fostering creativity and innovation. As you acquire knowledge and skills across multiple disciplines, you become more adept at recognizing patterns, drawing connections, and synthesizing information from various sources. As we have discussed throughout this book, the multidisciplinary perspective enables you to approach problems from unique angles, often leading to innovative solutions that might otherwise remain undiscovered.

The ability to communicate and collaborate with professionals from diverse fields is increasingly vital as interdisciplinary teamwork becomes the norm in many industries. And here's a bonus: The more you learn, the easier learning becomes.

To gain skills in multiple disciplines, we must adopt a proactive approach to our personal and professional development. This includes seeking out new experiences and embracing opportunities for growth, both within and beyond our current areas of expertise. By engaging in a variety of learning activities, such as reading, attending workshops and seminars, participating in online courses, and networking with professionals from other fields, you can build a broad knowledge base and a diverse skill set.

In addition to formal learning opportunities, it's essential for lifelong learners to cultivate habits of reflection and self-assessment. By regularly evaluating your progress and identifying areas for improvement, you can develop a deeper understanding of strengths and weaknesses, allowing you to make more informed decisions about your learning journey. Reflection also encourages critical thinking and self-awareness, essential skills for navigating the complexities of multidisciplinary environments. The good news is you will be testing yourself as you go (but don't worry: There's no final exam at the end). The bad news is you must hold yourself accountable as you learn.

The pursuit of lifelong learning and multidisciplinary expertise is a journey that requires dedication, curiosity, and adaptability. By embracing the challenges and opportunities that arise along the way, you can not only enhance your personal and professional lives but also contribute meaningfully to the broader world. In a time of unprecedented change and uncertainty, the commitment to being a lifelong learner has never been more important or more rewarding. But you have to have a plan, and time management is job one.

The Philadelphia Icon

When it comes to time management, the Philly boy in me always seems to come back to Benjamin Franklin. One of his lesser-known but still impressive achievements was his ability to manage his time effectively. Franklin's daily routine was a well-organized system that allowed him to maximize his productivity and achieve his goals.

Franklin was an early riser and believed in the adage, "Early to bed and early to rise, makes a man healthy, wealthy, and wise." He would wake up at 5:00 a.m. every day and begin his morning routine, which involved washing his face, brushing his teeth, and taking a cold bath. He believed that the cold bath invigorated his senses and prepared him for the day ahead.

After his morning routine, Franklin would spend an hour on what he called "powerful goodness." This involved reading and reflecting on a particular virtue that he wanted to focus on for the day. He had a list of thirteen virtues, including temperance, industry, and humility, which he would try to embody in his daily life.

Once he had completed his hour of reflection, Franklin would have breakfast and start his workday. He divided his day into three-hour blocks, with each block dedicated to a particular task. For example, from 8:00 a.m. to 11:00 a.m. he would work on his writing, research, or correspondence. He would then take a break and spend the next three hours on a different task, such as business or leisure activities.

Franklin's system of time management was not rigid, and he would adjust his schedule depending on his workload and other commitments. However, he believed that having a structured routine allowed him to be more productive and focused. In his autobiography, he wrote, "By the constant practice of certain virtues, we become habitual in them, and they become easy and delightful."

Franklin also recognized the importance of physical activity and made sure to incorporate exercise into his daily routine. He would take a walk every afternoon, which he believed helped him clear his mind and come up with new ideas. (And for physical activity, Frankliln apparently meant just movement, because if you ever saw a picture of Franklin, you know he was not a bodybuilder.)

In the evenings, Franklin would spend time with his family, have dinner, and engage in leisure activities such as reading, playing chess, or playing music. He believed that a balance between work and leisure was essential for a happy and fulfilling life.

How It's Done

The more you commit to being a Jack of all trades, the more you will absorb, and the more natural integration of ideas will become. Let's look at some hacks and methods that can support you in acquiring new knowledge and skills, enhancing your ability to think critically and creatively and, ultimately, thrive in multidisciplinary environments.

These approaches range from time-management techniques and memory-enhancing strategies to innovative learning tools and resources, all designed to empower you to become a more effective and resourceful learner.

Let's start with the six C's of learning:

- Commitment
- Calendaring
- Controlling Questions
- Chunking
- Collaboration
- Connections

Commitment

The first step in learning a new discipline is committing to it. This means that you need to be willing to put in the time and effort required to learn and master the subject. Learning a new discipline isn't something that's achieved overnight. It takes time and effort to build your knowledge. That's not something I can sugarcoat. But I can assure you that, once you dive in, learning will reward you so much that you will embrace it and find happiness.

The first step to successful learning is to set clear goals. Define your learning objectives and break them down into smaller, achievable milestones. By doing so, you can track your progress and stay motivated as you work towards your ultimate learning objective. Prioritization is also crucial. Determine which disciplines are most important or interesting to you and focus on them first. This will help you make the most efficient use of your learning time and stay motivated.

When you commit to learning a new discipline, it's important to set realistic goals. This means you need to identify what you want to achieve and then work towards those goals step-by-step. By setting achievable goals, you can avoid feeling overwhelmed and discouraged, helping you stay motivated and focused on your learning journey.

Once you've committed to the learning process, it's important to keep moving forward. Learning a new discipline is challenging, and there will be times when you feel like you're not making progress. Just remember that progress isn't always linear. There will be ups and downs, but as long as you keep moving forward, you will eventually achieve your goals.

One way to keep moving forward is to embrace challenges and setbacks as opportunities to learn and grow. When you encounter a difficult concept or problem, don't get discouraged. Instead, see it as a chance to expand your knowledge and skills. Take the time to reflect on what you've learned and how you can improve.

Calendaring

Another important aspect of committing to a new discipline is developing a consistent learning routine. This means you need to set aside time each day or week to study and practice. By creating a routine, you can establish a habit of learning that will help you make progress in the long run. Schedule your learning time on your calendar and commit to it. Scheduling dedicated learning time is essential to consistently ensuring time for learning and personal development.

The *Pomodoro Technique,* developed by Francesco Cirillo in the late 1980s, is a time-management method that breaks work into intervals, typically of 25 minutes, called *pomodoros.* After each pomodoro, a short break of five minutes is taken, and after completing four pomodoros, a longer break of 15-30 minutes is allowed. This method encourages deep focus, minimizes burnout, and helps maintain a sustainable work rhythm. Cirillo named these time blocks pomodoros because he used a kitchen timer that looked like a tomato. So there, I just squeezed in an Italian lesson: Pomodoro is Italian for tomato.

By breaking work into short intervals, you can focus on one task at a time without feeling overwhelmed. Before starting your work session, prioritize and organize your tasks. Determine which tasks require your full attention and deep focus, and which can be handled simultaneously or during breaks. Use the Pomodoro Technique for tasks that need undivided attention, and reserve multitasking for less demanding tasks. This allows you to work more efficiently and complete tasks with a higher level of accuracy. The frequent breaks help prevent burnout and increase motivation.

To use the Pomodoro technique, simply set a timer for 25 minutes and work on a single task until the timer goes off. Then take a short break, around five minutes, before starting the next 25-minute interval. After four intervals, take a longer break, around 15-30 minutes. These built-in breaks can be used for multitasking, allowing you to tackle less critical tasks or attend to small, routine responsibilities. This strategy helps maintain focus on primary tasks during pomodoros while ensuring that secondary tasks aren't neglected.

If you're struggling to concentrate on a single task during a pomodoro, you can switch to another task that requires a similar level of focus. This approach helps you maintain your momentum and prevents boredom or burnout. Adjust the length of pomodoros and breaks to suit your personal work style and the nature of your tasks. For example, if you find that multitasking is essential for your job, consider using shorter pomodoros with more frequent breaks to accommodate your need to switch between tasks.

As you use the Pomodoro Technique, you'll discover that it's effective in a variety of settings, including the workplace, school, and home. It can be especially helpful for those who struggle with staying focused or who tend to procrastinate. By breaking work into manageable chunks, the Pomodoro Technique can help you be more productive and feel less overwhelmed.

Controlling Questions

You can't contemplate a journey without asking where you want to go, so let's start this journey by asking a very specific question: What do you want to learn? To create controlling questions, focus on the how, why, and what if aspects of the subject. These questions will help you uncover the underlying principles and mechanisms at play. Keep a list of controlling questions for each subject or topic you're learning and revisit them regularly to refine your understanding and identify new areas of inquiry. Whether it's an unfamiliar language, a capability, or a career, setting the appropriate ambitions is the primary move to attaining victory.

When it comes to learning a new discipline, having focus and a narrow scope is incredibly beneficial. It allows you to dive deeply into a specific area of study and truly understand its intricacies. This type of focused learning can help you retain information more effectively and make connections between different concepts more easily.

Develop a narrow scope for learning a new discipline to identify your specific goals. What do you want to achieve by learning this discipline? Are you looking to gain a basic understanding, or do you want to become an expert? Once you have a clear idea of your goals, you can start to narrow the scope of your learning.

For example, if you want to learn how to code, you might choose to focus on one specific programming language, like Python. This allows you to become more proficient in that language, which can then serve as a foundation for learning more complex coding concepts later on.

Defining the controlling question means identifying and formulating the main question or problem that will guide your investigation or analysis of a particular topic. It's the central focus of any inquiry and helps clarify the purpose and scope of the investigation. It's the question that your research or analysis aims to answer, and it provides a framework for organizing and evaluating the evidence and arguments that will be presented.

In some cases, the controlling question may be explicitly stated, such as in a research proposal or thesis statement. In other cases, it may be implicit, but still guides the overall direction of the work.

Another benefit of a narrow scope is that it can help you stay motivated. When you have a clear sense of what you want to accomplish, it's easier to stay focused and avoid distractions. This is especially important when learning a new discipline, as it's easy to become overwhelmed by the sheer amount of available information.

Additionally, a narrow scope helps you track your progress more effectively. When you're focused on a specific area of study, you can set concrete goals and milestones that allow you to measure your progress. This is incredibly motivating and helps you stay on track.

Of course, there are also some potential downsides to having a narrow scope. For example, if you become too focused on one specific area you may miss out on important connections and interdisciplinary knowledge that can enhance your learning. Additionally, if you become too narrowly focused, you may start to lose sight of the bigger picture and miss out on important context and background information.

To mitigate these risks, it's helpful to periodically reassess your goals and scope as you learn. As you gain more knowledge and expertise, you may find that you need to broaden your scope in order to continue growing and developing. Additionally, it's useful to seek out opportunities to learn from other disciplines and connect your learning to the broader context.

Over my 35 years of legal practice, I always knew that the most important thing I could do is find the answer to "What is the controlling question?" That particular issue was the factor which would determine if the jury sided with me or not. What was the one thing that would stand between them and the verdict I desired?

So I applied that to the learning process. Define exactly what it is you wish to learn about a specific discipline and focus on that issue. The controlling question will tell you how much work you must do, and how deeply you have to dive.

How Do We Determine What We Need to Learn?

The *Pareto principle,* also known as the *80/20 rule,* states that 80% of effects come from 20% of causes. This widespread rule has multidisciplinary origins.

Vilfredo Pareto was a renowned Italian economist, sociologist, and philosopher who made significant contributions to the fields of economics, sociology, and political science. Born on July 15, 1848, in Paris, Pareto spent most of his life in Italy, where he made groundbreaking contributions to social sciences. His early work focused on engineering and mathematics, but he gradually shifted his focus to social sciences. He developed an interest in economics and began studying the works of classical economists such as Adam Smith and David Ricardo. In 1893, Pareto published his first significant work, *Cours d'Économie Politique,* which established his reputation as an economist.

Pareto's most significant contribution to social sciences was the Pareto principle, which he formulated while studying income distribution in Italy. Pareto observed that 80% of the land in Italy was owned by 20% of the population, and this pattern was repeated across other areas, such as wealth distribution and industrial production. Pareto concluded that this was a universal phenomenon that applied to all aspects of society.

His concept of the Pareto principle has been widely applied in various fields, such as business, management, and marketing. His ideas on income distribution and the elite have also influenced political and social movements, such as socialism and communism.

Vilfredo Pareto was a multidisciplinary scholar who made significant contributions to social sciences. His legacy lives on, and his ideas continue to influence contemporary thinking and research in social sciences.

The Pareto principle is a major step toward becoming an expert at anything. You don't need to learn everything, just the 20% that matters. So, take a deep breath and realize that *you don't need to know everything to be an expert*. The Pareto principle recognizes that 80% of the effects come from 20% of the causes. This means that in any given situation, there are only a few things that really matter.

Let's say you want to learn a new discipline. Instead of trying to absorb every piece of information available, you should focus on the 20% of knowledge that will give you the most value. Your goals should be specific, measurable, achievable, relevant, and time bound. For example, instead of saying, "I want to learn French," you might say, "I want to be able to hold a conversation in French within six months." This narrows the scope. When I wanted to learn woodworking in my younger years, I chose the narrow path of *finish carpentry in cabinet making*. Give me a cabinet and I'll make it look good; just don't ask me to build the whole darn thing!

My goals were focused. Applying the Perato principle will maximize your efforts and help you achieve your goals more efficiently by directing your energy towards the most important things rather than spreading yourself too thin. You'll be surprised by how much more you can achieve with less effort.

Chunking

Setting goals is easy; achieving them is a different story. It's important to ensure that the goals you set are achievable and realistic. Redefine the topic until you can create a path to the next step. But how do you do that?

Restructuring a topic involves breaking it into smaller, more manageable pieces, or chunks, and analyzing each part separately. In doing so, you gain a deeper understanding of the topic and its underlying concepts, identifying connections and relationships between different elements.

For example, if you were studying a complex scientific theory, you might break it into its key components and examine each one in detail. This could involve researching the theory's historical context, analyzing the scientific evidence that supports it, and exploring alternative theories that have been proposed. Restructuring a topic in this way can also help you identify gaps in your understanding and focus your learning on areas that require further attention. This helps develop a more thorough understanding of the topic and points you toward a more informed and critical perspective.

At its core, chunking is based on the idea that our working memory can only hold a limited amount of information at any given time. Research suggests that the average person can hold between five to nine pieces of knowledge in their working memory. This means that if we are presented with a large amount of information all at once, we're likely to struggle with processing and remembering it.

Chunking helps overcome this limitation by breaking information into smaller, more meaningful units. By grouping related pieces of information together, we can reduce the cognitive load on our working memory, making it easier to process and remember the information.

For example, if you're trying to memorize a long list of numbers such as 123456789, it may be easier to break it into smaller chunks such as 12-34-56-78-9. By doing this, you reduce the number of items you need to remember from nine to five, making the information easier to retain.

Chunking can also be applied to more complex information such as scientific concepts, historical events, or mathematical formulas, helping us better understand how ideas relate to one another and creating a mental framework for organizing the information.

In addition to breaking information into smaller pieces, chunking can also be used to link new information to prior knowledge, a technique known as *elaborative chunking*.

If you're trying to learn a new language, you can use elaborative chunking by associating new vocabulary with familiar objects or experiences. If you're learning the word for dog in a new language, you can associate it with the image of your own pet dog, making it easier to remember and recall the word in the future.

Chunking is a powerful learning technique that can help us overcome the limitations of our working memory and improve our ability to process, retain, and apply new information. By breaking down information into smaller, more manageable pieces and linking it to prior knowledge, we can create a more efficient and effective learning process. Whether you're a student, a professional, or a lifelong learner, incorporating chunking into your learning routine can help you achieve greater success in your academic and personal pursuits.

Collaboration

Learning isn't just something we do with books, YouTube, or Audible. The best learning we can accomplish is through mentors and experts who can provide valuable insights and help you learn from their experiences. Joining study groups or forums to collaborate with others interested in multidisciplinary learning is another effective way to share knowledge and ideas. Collaboration allows you to dive into a discipline and do, not simply think.

Learning by doing, also known as *experiential learning*, is a powerful method of education that involves learning through practical, hands-on experiences rather than just reading about or listening to concepts. David A. Kolb, in his 1983 book *Experiential Learning: Experience as the Source of Learning and Development*, states that this type of learning is a powerful tool that can help you develop a deeper understanding of concepts, improve problem-solving skills, and increase retention rates.

Kolb, a professor of organizational behavior at the Weatherhead School of Management at Case Western Reserve

University, discusses a four-stage learning cycle consisting of *concrete experience, reflective observation, abstract conceptualization,* and *active experimentation.* The cycle starts with a concrete experience, such as a hands-on activity or a real-life situation. Learners then reflect on this experience, considering what they observed and what they learned from it. They then move to the abstract conceptualization stage, where they analyze and make connections between their experiences and abstract concepts. Finally, they engage in active experimentation, applying what they have learned to new situations.

Collaborating with experts in a specific discipline can enable experiential learning that helps you develop a deeper understanding of concepts. By engaging in hands-on experiences, learners can see firsthand how concepts apply to real-world situations, helping to create a more meaningful and lasting understanding of the material.

Experiential learning also increases retention rates. Studies have shown that people remember only 10% of what they read and 20% of what they hear but retain up to 90% of what they do. This is because experiential learning engages multiple senses and requires active participation, helping to create more neural pathways in the brain.

By collaborating with experts to get a hands-on approach, you'll experience a much deeper understanding of what you're learning. You'll see its application in the real world as well as discover greater connections that you might have otherwise overlooked by being simply "book smart." The feedback you'll receive will create a dynamic learning experience that can only be developed by having a mentor, coach, or peer challenging you with practical application and testing. Feedback can help you identify areas where you need to improve and provide you with valuable insights and advice.

Connections

In the world of knowledge, various disciplines are often perceived as distinct entities, each with its own set of rules and principles. While traditional education systems have primarily focused on compartmentalized learning, there is growing evidence that looking for *connections* between subjects can yield immense benefits.

Our brains are wired to seek patterns and relationships. It's a fundamental part of our nature. In fact, it's one of the key reasons why we've been able to make such incredible advances in science, technology, and countless other fields. When we actively look for connections between topics, we're doing more than just satisfying our innate curiosity. We're tapping into a powerful learning strategy that can help us gain a deeper understanding of the world around us.

How does this actually work? Let's say you're studying two seemingly unrelated subjects—say, art history and chemistry. At first glance you might think they have nothing in common. But when you start exploring the connections, you'll find that the materials and pigments used by artists are derived from chemical substances. Suddenly, you're seeing these two subjects in a whole new light. That's the magic of making connections.

Finding connections can make learning more enjoyable, too. When we're able to relate new information to something we already know it becomes more meaningful and easier to remember. Plus, the more connections we make, the more opportunities we have to get excited about the learning process. It's a win-win situation!

Interconnected learning emphasizes the importance of understanding the relationships between different subjects, fostering a holistic approach to education. It encourages you to think critically and analytically about the links between seemingly unrelated topics. As a result, you'll develop a more comprehensive understanding of the world and be better equipped to make informed decisions and solve complex problems.

Relating new information to previously learned material makes you more likely to remember and internalize concepts. The process of identifying connections enables you to develop a more profound understanding of a subject as you actively engage in the synthesis and integration of ideas.

One of the key benefits of interconnected learning is the ease with which learners can transfer knowledge from one domain to another. By identifying connections between subjects, you become adept at applying knowledge and skills from one area to solve problems in another. Frankly, my experience shows that the more connections you find, the more excited you become about hopping from discipline to discipline to discover things that are new.

When you start to see how interconnected the world is, you'll find a great boost in motivation and engagement as you discover the relevance and real-world applications of the subjects you're learning, making you more naturally inclined to want to know more. This heightened engagement not only makes the learning process more enjoyable, it also increases the likelihood of long-term success.

When you actively seek connections between subjects, you stimulate your creative and innovative thinking. All the benefits that I've discussed in the previous chapters become clearer and come more naturally in everything you do. And as you combine ideas from various fields, you'll be more likely to develop novel insights and solutions to complex problems. This interdisciplinary approach to learning nurtures creativity and promotes a growth mindset as you become more open to exploring new ideas and taking risks.

By following the concepts laid out in this chapter, your learning will be much deeper and more engaging. Your subconscious will develop confidence that will drive you every step of the way. And, as you'll see in the next chapter, taking on this learning with self-motivation and confidence will help you tackle any hesitation or doubt that you may have of your new expertise.

JOURNEY MILEPOSTS

- **Lifelong Learning and Adaptability:** Considering the narrative on lifelong learning, think about how being a "Jack of all trades" can be beneficial in our rapidly changing world. Do you believe that adaptability and a multidisciplinary approach offer a competitive advantage in today's job market? Can you recall a time when your varied knowledge or quick learning ability gave you an edge?

- **Challenging Experts:** Reflect on the process we went through to challenge experts in various fields. Have you ever had to quickly learn a subject to hold your ground in a discussion or work setting? What methods did you employ to grasp the essentials and what might you have done differently knowing the strategies outlined here?

- **The Six C's of Learning:** Take a moment to assess the six C's: Commitment, Calendaring, Controlling Questions, Chunking, Collaboration, and Connections. Which of these resonates most with your personal learning style, and which might you want to develop further? How can you integrate these methods into your current learning or work routines?

- **Importance of the Controlling Question:** The concept of having a controlling question to guide focus and understanding of a subject is highlighted. Can you think of an instance where identifying a central issue or question could have steered a project or learning endeavor more effectively for you? Moving forward, how might you employ this strategy in personal or professional pursuits?

- **The Pareto Principle in Learning:** The Pareto Principle suggests that 80% of results come from 20% of efforts. In the context of learning, this could mean that a focused 20% of effort or knowledge could yield 80% of the desired outcome. How have you seen the Pareto Principle manifest in your own learning experiences?

- **The Art of Chunking:** Chunking breaks information into smaller, digestible bits to aid memory and comprehension. How has chunking helped you in your personal or professional studies? Can you think of a situation where chunking might not be effective? How can we ensure that, while breaking things into smaller pieces, we don't lose the bigger picture or context?

- **The Power of Collaboration:** Collaborative and experiential learning, as suggested by David A. Kolb, emphasizes the importance of hands-on experiences and feedback. How has collaboration with peers or mentors enriched your own learning journey? In which disciplines or subjects do you think collaboration is most beneficial?

- **Interdisciplinary Connections:** Interconnected learning promotes a holistic understanding by highlighting connections between seemingly disparate subjects. Can you recall an instance where making a connection between two people deepened your understanding of both? How can you be more proactive in drawing connections across disciplines?

14

The Instant Expert and Overcoming Imposter Syndrome

*It is possible to fly without motors, but not
without knowledge and skill.*
— Wilbur Wright

When you're learning in multiple lanes, there's a tendency to feel like you're a bit of an imposter. I'm going tell you right now that this is natural because you're not as deep of an expert in any given area as others may be, which creates a sense of insecurity. Also, no matter what you've read in this book, there's that haunting voice in the back of your mind that keeps reminding you that a Jack of all trades is a master of none. That's a hard voice to ignore. Even with everything that you've read and learned, there's always that tiger mom in the back of your mind that pushes you.

You are not alone. Many of us experience imposter syndrome, especially when we're multidisciplinary and constantly learning new things. Fortunately, imposter syndrome can be identified, understood, and overcome.

Unmasking Imposter Syndrome

Have you ever felt like you don't deserve your accomplishments, that you're a fraud, or that people are going to find out you're not as competent as they thought you were? If so, you may be experiencing imposter syndrome, a psychological pattern in which an individual doubts their abilities and feels like a fraud despite evidence of their accomplishments, often creating an irrational fear of being exposed as a fraud or of not living up to expectations. It's a common feeling, especially among high achievers or those in positions of authority.

Other common symptoms of imposter syndrome include worrying that you've just been lucky, or that you don't really deserve your success. Additionally, you may be afraid of failing or making mistakes, causing you to procrastinate or avoid challenges. Perfectionism is another common symptom of imposter syndrome, and you may feel like you always need to be perfect in everything you do. Some people with imposter syndrome overwork themselves as a way to prove their worth, while others constantly doubt their abilities and seek validation from others. There are many potential causes of imposter syndrome, including personal and societal pressures, as well as past experiences that have led to a lack of confidence.

Imposter syndrome can also stem from a variety of factors including personality traits, upbringing, work environment, and previous failures. For instance, individuals who are perfectionists or anxiety-prone may be more likely to experience imposter syndrome. Similarly, individuals who were raised in households that placed a lot of pressure on their children to succeed, or emphasized achievement, may be more likely to experience imposter syndrome. A highly competitive or critical work environment can also make individuals feel like they're not good enough. Additionally, individuals who have experienced failure in the past may be more likely to feel like a fraud when they achieve success. All these factors can contribute to the development of imposter syndrome, which can affect an individual's self-esteem and confidence.

The reality is that imposter syndrome is often based on inaccurate self-perceptions. Individuals who experience imposter syndrome may discount their successes, attribute their accomplishments to luck or external factors, and underestimate their abilities. These negative self-perceptions can lead to anxiety, depression, and feelings of inadequacy.

Have Skin in the Game

We are all constantly looking for ways to improve ourselves, to become better at what we do, and to reach our goals. And we'd all like to avoid imposter syndrome. In these pursuits, we often overlook one crucial factor that could make all the difference: having skin in the game.

What do I mean by that? I mean being fully invested in your own learning and growth. I mean taking ownership of your journey and not just relying on others to guide you. To truly become an expert in your field, you need to teach and test yourself.

Teaching others is a great way to solidify your knowledge and understanding of a subject. When you explain something to someone else, you are forced to simplify and clarify your own thoughts which can help you identify any gaps in your understanding and fill them in. Additionally, when you teach someone else, you receive feedback that can help you improve even further.

Testing yourself is equally important. By setting challenges and goals, you can identify your strengths and weaknesses, helping you create a roadmap for your continued learning and development. You can focus on improving in areas where you are weak and use your strengths to your advantage.

But what is the driving force behind having skin in the game? It's your *why*. Why are you doing this? What do you have to lose if you don't accomplish your goal? When you have a strong reason behind your actions, you are much more likely to stay committed and see things through to the end.

Skin in the Game and a Pan on the Stove

As I've gone through life, learning has become second nature. Let me tell you about my journey in the restaurant business—it's a wild ride! When I first had the crazy idea of opening a restaurant, I had no clue where to even start. But I'm the kind of person who loves to learn new things and challenge myself, so I decided to jump right in and see where it took me.

I went to a friend's restaurant and told him my plans. He laughed and told me I was crazy, but he wasn't going to turn down an intern. So, starting the following Friday, I worked in his kitchen as his sous chef. Every Friday night, for nearly six years, I prepped food. On good nights, he'd actually let me cook. But honestly, I think I learned the most when he yelled at me for not cutting the parsley finely enough. Apparently, parsley can change an entire recipe—who knew?

Let's look at my learning approach in action.

First, I decided that the controlling question was that I wished to learn how to cook southern Italian cuisine. That was exactly what Frank served, so I chose his restaurant. I loved what he cooked, so I chose him as my focus. I wanted to cook like Frank. My scope was narrow.

Frank helped me chunk the process by starting with cutting up herbs, then cutting the meat, then prepping sauces and soups, and eventually every step along the way was covered. There is almost no better analogy for chunking than looking at a recipe. Everything is broken into measurable chunks and the process is a clean roadmap. Frank was an amazing teacher, and I was a dedicated student.

By committing to Frank that I would help him on Friday nights, the action plan was in place. No matter how tired I was, I left my law office and went to his restaurant. My family also committed to eat at that restaurant every Friday night, but they got to do so at the table in the kitchen. They thought that was cool… and so did I.

Frank was willing to teach me, and I was willing to learn. Therefore, the plan was moving forward because I would not have ever allowed Frank to be left holding the bag on Friday night. I showed up!

He was relying on my help on the busiest night of the week, and I was locked in. I had no choice but to move forward.

What was my skin in the game? My money was at stake. I wanted to open a restaurant.

There was no way I was doing that until I saw every aspect of what Frank did. Over my "apprenticeship" I had the opportunity to learn how to cook, to observe the process of operating the kitchen, how the floor was managed, and how even the most mundane of orders were placed with the food supplier. Frank knew I wanted to be in the restaurant business, so I was committed to learning, he was committed to teaching, and we both knew the only way we would open a restaurant was if we were locked in. We were a match made in restaurant heaven! And understanding the process I used to gain this expertise has helped me avoid imposter syndrome. I know what I know, and I know how I learned it. I'm not an imposter. I'm the real deal.

After five and a half years of learning and working, we finally opened our own restaurant together, the Tuscan Bistro. It was a high-end Italian restaurant with 30 tables. And guess what? We were packed every Thursday through Saturday! I was the maître d' and floor manager, and it was exhausting, but also so much fun. Of course, there were some hiccups along the way. One night, our head chef and my friend had a fight and I had to step up and run the kitchen. It was crazy! I kept the kitchen running while the wait staff convinced the warring chefs to come back into the building. Thank God for those Friday nights where I learned how to cook. I knew our menu and I knew our recipes.

That only happened one night, but I assure you, if you've ever heard stories about how temperamental chefs can be… Those stories are not reserved for Gordon Ramsay. Compared to what I've seen, he's a pussycat.

Recognize Your Accomplishments

Imposter syndrome is not a sign of weakness or incompetence. In fact, imposter syndrome is a sign of self-awareness and a desire for excellence. It shows that you care about your work, and you want to do your best.

Recognizing imposter syndrome requires a willingness to be honest with yourself about your feelings and your thought patterns. You may feel like you aren't good enough, that you're a fraud, or that you don't deserve your success. These feelings can be intense and overwhelming, but they are a natural part of the human experience. Recognize them.

Acknowledge Your Feelings

Acknowledging your feelings means that you allow yourself to feel them without judgment or self-criticism. You can practice mindfulness techniques, such as meditation, to help you observe your thoughts and emotions without getting caught up in them. You can also journal your thoughts and feelings to gain insight into your patterns and triggers.

Once you acknowledge your feelings, you can begin to challenge your thoughts and beliefs. Imposter syndrome is often rooted in deep-seated beliefs about ourselves, such as *I'm not smart enough* or *I'm not talented enough*. These beliefs are often based on inaccurate or incomplete information, and they can be changed with practice.

One way to challenge your thoughts is to ask yourself if they are true, and if there is evidence to support them. You can also reframe your thoughts in a more positive and empowering way. For example, instead of thinking *I don't belong here,* you can reframe it as *I worked hard to get here, and I deserve to be here.* It can make all the difference in the world.

Embrace Your Authentic Self

It's important to embrace your authentic self and recognize your unique strengths and talents. Imposter syndrome can make you feel like you need to be perfect or that you need to live up to other people's expectations. However, the reality is that we all have flaws and imperfections. It's what makes us human. Embrace your authenticity and focus on your strengths, rather than trying to be someone else.

It's also important to remember that everyone makes mistakes and has room for improvement. No one is perfect, and you are no exception. Instead of focusing on your mistakes, focus on the lessons learned and how you can improve in the future. By reframing your mistakes as learning opportunities, you can shift your mindset from one of inadequacy to one of growth.

In short, by recognizing that imposter syndrome is a real phenomenon and that many people experience it, you can begin to challenge your negative thoughts and beliefs, and embrace your authentic self. Remember, you are capable, deserving, and worthy of your success, and you have the power to overcome imposter syndrome and achieve your goals.

Seek Support

Another way to overcome imposter syndrome is to seek support from others. Talk to colleagues, friends, or family members who can provide encouragement and perspective. Share your concerns and fears with others and be open to feedback and support. Others can provide a more objective view of your abilities and accomplishments than you can.

It may also be helpful to seek a mentor who can provide guidance and support. A mentor can offer advice and share their own experiences of overcoming imposter syndrome. They can also help you identify areas where you need to improve and provide resources to help you develop your skills.

Challenge Your Self-Doubt

To overcome imposter syndrome, it's important to challenge your self-doubt and negative self-perceptions. One way to do this is to identify the specific thoughts or beliefs that contribute to your imposter syndrome. Record these thoughts and challenge them with evidence to the contrary. For example, if you believe you're not qualified for a new project, write down all the skills and experiences that make you a good fit for the project.

It may also be helpful to practice self-compassion. Treat yourself with the same kindness and understanding that you would offer to a friend. Remember: Everyone experiences self-doubt and it's a natural part of the learning process.

Embrace Your Multidisciplinary Nature

Finally, it's important to embrace your multidisciplinary nature and see it as a strength. Your diverse skills and experiences can provide a unique perspective and make you a valuable asset to any team or project. Instead of feeling like you don't have enough expertise in any one area, see yourself as a versatile and adaptable learner who can take on new challenges and succeed.

Imposter syndrome can be a significant obstacle to overcome, but with awareness and intentional effort, it is possible to move past it. As a multidisciplinary learner, it's especially important to recognize and acknowledge your accomplishments, seek support from others, challenge your self-doubt, and embrace your unique strengths. Remember that you are not a fraud, and your worth is not defined by any one accomplishment or area of expertise. You are capable of learning and growing in new areas, and your multidisciplinary nature is a strength to be celebrated. You can achieve great things, and with perseverance and self-compassion, you can overcome imposter syndrome and achieve your goals.

JOURNEY MILEPOSTS

- **The Multidisciplinary Nature:** Reflect on the times you've felt like a "Jack of all trades" but worried you might not be a "master of any." In today's complex world, how can being multidisciplinary be a strength, rather than a weakness? Think about how your diverse skill set can be an advantage in various situations.

- **Recognizing vs. Accepting Imposter Syndrome:** Imposter syndrome is common, but that doesn't make it any less challenging. Reflect on a moment when you felt it most intensely. What triggered it, and how did you cope? Now, armed with the knowledge from this chapter, how might you approach similar feelings differently in the future? Start to realize that you're not an expert in everything, but a knowledgeable generalist who is an expert at integration. Overcome imposter syndrome by embracing your superpower.

- **The Role of External Validation:** How much weight do we give to external feedback, praises, or critiques in shaping our self-perception? How can we balance seeking external validation with cultivating intrinsic self-worth?

- **Having Skin in the Game:** My experiences in the restaurant venture emphasize the importance of commitment and immersion in one's journey. How do hands-on experiences reinforce our learnings and solidify our confidence in a given field?

- **Challenge Internal Narratives:** In our moments of doubt, how might we develop tools or practices to challenge and reframe the internal narratives that fuel imposter syndrome? How do we differentiate between constructive self-reflection and debilitating self-doubt?

- **The Power of Community and Mentorship:** We often believe our internal struggles are unique to us when, in reality, many others may share the same feelings. Discuss the importance of finding a mentor or a supportive community. How can sharing experiences and seeking feedback combat the feelings of imposter syndrome? Consider a moment when someone else's perspective provided clarity to your self-doubt.

DO MORE

15

Multidisciplinary Teams: Orchestrating Success in Diverse Teams

One can state, without exaggeration, that the observation of and the search for similarities and differences are the basis of all human knowledge.
— Alfred Nobel

The use of multidisciplinary teams has ancient roots, but it has evolved and gained prominence over time as society recognized the power of combining diverse perspectives and skills to tackle complex challenges and drive innovation. Today, multidisciplinary teams are prevalent not only in healthcare and research but also in various industries and organizations, where they continue to play a vital role in problem-solving and innovation.

The traditional silos that once separated departments proved to be barriers to progress, hindering collaboration and stifling innovation. Our problems and challenges are rarely limited to a single department or area of expertise. Instead, they often require input and collaboration from a diverse group of experts with different skills and perspectives.

In order to succeed, businesses need to break down those walls and embrace a more interdisciplinary approach to problem-solving. For those who were willing to adapt and evolve, the possibilities were endless. That's when the concept of the multidisciplinary team was born.

Multidisciplinary Teams

Multidisciplinary teams are made up of individuals from different fields and disciplines who come together to work on a shared project or goal. These teams leverage the diverse skills and knowledge of their members to create innovative solutions that wouldn't be possible with a single-discipline approach. Much like my earlier metaphorical fruit-based dishes, multidisciplinary teams are akin to a potluck dinner where individuals from various disciplines come together, each bringing their unique expertise to the table.

In this collaborative setting, team members retain their distinct identities, much like the separate fruits in a salad. Their diverse knowledge and skills are valuable ingredients that contribute to a broader understanding and comprehensive problem-solving. These teams are excellent when you need a wide range of expertise to address multifaceted challenges while still preserving the integrity of each discipline within the group.

My first exposure to multidisciplinary teams was in the early days of my career as a prosecutor of white-collar crime. I was the acting chief deputy of the attorney general's Medicaid fraud unit for Pennsylvania which investigated doctors, hospitals, and nursing homes that defrauded the Medicaid system. To increase our investigative ability and understanding of the various professions, we got together monthly with a team of over 40 prosecutors, accountants, analysts, auditors, medical professionals, and statisticians to review the methods being used by criminals to create billing systems that stole Medicaid money. The input of every person at the table was valuable. Only together could we understand the minds of the criminals we were investigating. We knew that a multidisciplinary approach allowed us to see connections and possibilities better than a sole investigator could.

I should also mention that some of the white-collar criminals we dealt with were geniuses and it took a room of 40-plus people to undo what they created. And it doesn't escape me that some of those criminals weren't just doctors, they were multidisciplinary. They were good at what they did because they were extremely worldly and well-versed in a lot of areas. But, by working together and sharing our expertise, our multidisciplinary team was able to break down traditional silos and bring new and creative ideas to the table. This approach allowed us a lot of latitude to dig into and uncover major fraud in the healthcare system. However, this approach also presented its own unique challenges, such as communication barriers and differences in work styles and priorities. We'll get to those challenges soon. For now, let's look at…

The Many Benefits of Multidisciplinary Teams

Through my experience in the courtroom, I knew that the work our team did had to be virtually flawless. As prosecutors, we couldn't arrest innocent people. Therefore, we knew that we needed to cover all possible angles. The only way to make sure this was done was to pull our experts from various fields and hold robust discussions to look at the options. Keep in mind that we needed a level of certainty that ensured a case could be tried beyond a reasonable doubt, and many times we had no idea what the challenges were going to be because the defense attorneys weren't required to tell us their strategies. We had to be prepared for every possibility and every surprise.

The input and analysis of people from diverse backgrounds became essential to everything I did. I needed the perspective of accountants just as much as I needed the perspective of doctors. I needed the perspective of insurance adjusters just as much as I needed the perspective of law-enforcement officials. It was a truly multidisciplinary endeavor.

One of the most significant benefits of the multidisciplinary approach is the greater knowledge and expertise that it can bring to a problem or project. By bringing together experts from different fields, a multidisciplinary team can access a wider range of knowledge and skills, which can lead to more effective solutions. Multidisciplinary thinking helps you to see the world in a new way.

Another benefit of multidisciplinary teams is that they can lead to increased creativity and innovation. Different perspectives and ideas can lead to new and innovative solutions to problems, which can positively impact the outcome of a project. When experts from different fields work together, they can challenge each other's assumptions and come up with new and innovative ideas that they would not have thought of on their own. This is particularly beneficial in fields that are rapidly changing and require constant innovation to stay competitive.

By pooling together different areas of expertise, a multidisciplinary team can approach problems from multiple angles and come up with more effective solutions, especially in complex and multi-dimensional problems that require multiple skills and perspectives to solve. For example, a team that includes experts from both medicine and psychology may be better equipped to develop a treatment plan for a patient with a mental health condition. By combining the knowledge and skills of different fields, a multidisciplinary team can identify and address all the factors that contribute to a problem, resulting in more comprehensive and effective solutions.

With a diverse range of knowledge and expertise, the multidisciplinary approach leads to more informed decisions and minimizes the risk of overlooking important factors. This is particularly important in fields where decisions have significant consequences, such as healthcare or finance. When team members from different fields work together, they can bring different perspectives and knowledge to the table, helping the team to identify and weigh all the relevant factors.

Additionally, as we will explore later, when there are multiple disciplines in play, the ability to think through a problem takes on a life of its own. What we might normally see as a quick decision is actually forced into a process so that a more thorough decision results. When people are working in single lanes, and someone from another lane comes into play, it's like a smack on the side of the head, because the decision needs to be thought out and explained so that every person in every lane grasps it. It doesn't allow us to be lazy. As you'll see later, it's human nature to opt for the easy. Whether it's an individual or a team, multidisciplinary thinking and analysis forces disruption. When this happens, new solutions and new discoveries occur.

Getting on the Same Page

When team members are able to communicate effectively and collaborate efficiently, they can work together to solve problems and achieve goals. Additionally, a multidisciplinary team can foster a culture of learning and growth where team members can learn from each other's diverse perspectives and expertise, leading to personal and professional growth.

Once, when I was working on a large real estate land-dispute case, I was dealing with an engineer, a surveyor, a contractor, and (obviously) lawyers. To say that communication among this group was a challenge is a colossal understatement. We weren't even in court, and my clients were pointing fingers at each other, and blame was being cast among my witnesses.

This was one of the first times that I truly began to embrace my multidisciplinary nature. As I sat at a table, trying to get everyone on the same page, I quickly realized that I had been involved, at some point in my life, in every one of those careers. Once I began to speak to each individual on their own terms, and in their language, I was able to herd the cats and get them on the same page. Simply put, whether it was the surveyor, the engineer, the contractor, or the lawyers, they all spoke a different language, and I had enough background in each of those areas to be able to talk their language. I brought everyone together, we forged ahead, and we prevailed.

This underscores my point: Multidisciplinary people and teams are able to adapt more easily to changing circumstances and new information, which is beneficial in dynamic environments. When team members are exposed to different ways of thinking and working, they can become more adaptable and flexible in their approach to problem-solving and communication. This can help the team work together more smoothly, respond more quickly and effectively to changing circumstances, and take advantage of new opportunities. Additionally, multidisciplinary teams are more resilient to disruptions and setbacks, as they have a wider range of skills and knowledge to draw upon. Since people who are trained in multiple disciplines have the ability to think in different ways, and in different lanes, every situation can take on a life of its own. Since multidisciplinary individuals are significantly more prone to be lifelong learners, every situation becomes a learning process. Accordingly, they do not have myopia and are more prepared to shift their thinking at any time. The beauty of being multidisciplinary is that you can adapt to any situation.

The combination of different skills and expertise in a multidisciplinary team can lead to more efficient and productive work processes, ultimately generating better results. When team members are able to work together effectively and efficiently, they can accomplish more in less time. Additionally, the diverse range of knowledge and skills in a multidisciplinary team can lead to more efficient problem-solving, as team members can rely on each other's expertise to overcome obstacles. Additionally, multidisciplinary teams can lead to improved communication and collaboration, better decision-making, increased adaptability, and enhanced productivity. These benefits can help organizations tackle complex challenges and drive innovation, leading to improved outcomes and increased competitiveness.

An individual with multidisciplinary skills as a leader can play an important role in harnessing the potential of multidisciplinary teams to solve complex challenges and drive innovation in the organization by implementing and coordinating all of the various lanes of thought in one direction.

Multidisciplinary Teams, Multiple Challenges

But while multidisciplinary teams can bring numerous benefits to an organization, they also come with their own set of challenges. Communication barriers, conflicting priorities, power imbalances, role confusion, limited understanding of other disciplines, time-consuming coordination, and dependency on specific members are among the most significant hurdles. Communication barriers are one of the main challenges that multidisciplinary teams face. To overcome this, effective communication strategies and tools need to be implemented.

Conflicts and disagreements may arise due to different goals and priorities. Establishing a shared vision and goals for the team and aligning incentives and rewards can help overcome this challenge. Some disciplines may have more expertise or decision-making power than others, leading to dominance and a lack of equal participation. Encouraging equal participation and providing opportunities for all team members to contribute can help. Team members may not understand the roles and responsibilities of each discipline, which can lead to confusion and inefficiencies. To overcome this, the team leader should clearly define the roles and responsibilities of each member and provide training and resources to help each member understand the methods and practices of others. Coordinating schedules and availability of team members from different disciplines can be time-consuming and challenging. Using technology to facilitate coordination and collaboration can help overcome this. Finally, the team may become dependent on specific members with specialized knowledge, leading to limitations in decision-making and problem-solving. Providing opportunities for team members to learn from each other can help ensure that the team is not overly dependent on specific members.

Multidisciplinary teams are an effective way to tackle complex challenges and drive innovation but, as you see, they also come with their own challenges. By understanding these challenges and implementing strategies to address them, the team leader can ensure that the team works effectively and efficiently and can overcome obstacles to achieve success.

As we consider juggling the specifics and details of each individual discipline, it needs to be pointed out that an individual who understands, possesses, and also personally juggles the uniqueness of each discipline is the solution to the problems of communication barriers, conflicting priorities, power imbalances, role confusion, limited understanding of other disciplines, time-consuming coordination, and dependency on specific members. This person can bring together different expertise, techniques, and strategies, helping teams identify the most effective approaches to collaborate and understand one other. Multidisciplinary minds can bridge gaps in understanding, motivate diverse groups, and build constructive dialogue. They can also act as a mediator, providing unbiased perspectives and identifying common ground.

Collectively, these teams use their problem-solving capabilities to break through obstacles, such as finding alternative ways of approaching a situation, making sure that everybody's contributions are recognized, and exploring all possibilities. Through this, teams can establish and maintain productive relationships, allowing them to better respond to external and internal changes, resolve conflicts in a more efficient way, and foster creative thinking.

My Pet Peeve

Yes, you read that right. I have a pet peeve about multidisciplinary teams. How the team is formed will ultimately control its results. Most leaders do not know how to get the most out of a collaborative team. Diagnosing medical problems will always be well handled by a *multidisciplinary team*, but forward-thinking companies, and people looking to take on the future, need to allow their teams to take on a life of their own. Doing that will push the team so that cross-disciplinary magic happens on a regular basis.

It's only when the disciplines intersect that you'll experience magnificent, awe-inspiring results. Without a skilled leader, someone might miss that magic moment.

JOURNEY MILEPOSTS

- **Revisiting the Traditional Approach:** How do you think the traditional ways of problem-solving and teamwork fall short in today's complex organizational landscape? Can a single department or discipline efficiently tackle these multifaceted challenges? Think of a specific situation and consider what other fields might contribute to a more effective solution where they brought into the loop.

- **Value of Diversity in Complex Projects:** In your experience, how has the inclusion of individuals from diverse backgrounds influenced the success of a project? What new perspectives or solutions emerged as a result?

- **Challenges and Triumphs:** While multidisciplinary teams offer a plethora of benefits, they are not without their own unique challenges. How do communication barriers and differences in work styles/priorities present hurdles? How can these be mitigated? Reflect upon how the multidisciplinary leader can solve these problems.

- **The Role of a Multidisciplinary Leader:** How can an individual with expertise in multiple fields act as a catalyst in ensuring that multidisciplinary teams work cohesively and effectively? Consider the balance of harnessing diverse perspectives while providing clear direction.

- **Beyond Teams—the Individual:** As we transition to understanding the individual multidisciplinary mindset in the next chapter, ponder upon how such individuals apply their broad range of skills in decision-making. How might they see patterns, connections, and opportunities that others might overlook? Can you provide examples where such an individual played a pivotal role in bridging understanding or overcoming challenges?

- **Boosting Creativity and Innovation:** How do diverse team members challenge one other's assumptions and perspectives? Can you think of a situation where this led to a groundbreaking idea or a novel approach?

16

A Productive Mix: The Power of Collaborative Teams

Individual commitment to a group effort—that is what makes a team work, a company work, a society work, a civilization work.
— Vince Lombardi

The power of collaborative teams is a non-negotiable tool to use as we move into the future. The world is moving way too fast to keep everything in silos. Teams exist in various forms, including interdisciplinary, cross-functional, and multidisciplinary ones, each distinguished by its unique purpose and composition. Much as we said earlier about the various forms of thinking, let's take a look at what the actual "team" concept looks like in each area:

- Cross-functional teams involve members from different functional areas within an organization, working together to achieve specific goals or projects.

- Interdisciplinary teams bring together individuals from diverse fields or disciplines to address complex problems, with a focus on integrating knowledge from multiple areas.

- Multidisciplinary teams consist of experts from various disciplines who work independently within their domains, collaborating by sharing their specialized insights and contributions to achieve a common objective.

Now that those formal distinctions are out of the way, whatever you call your team, it's up to you to set goals and direction. For the purposes of this book, the label you put on your collaborative team is not as important as how you manage it, how you define it, and how it operates.

In this chapter, we'll explore the goals that bind collaborative teams together and understand how to harness the collective potential they offer. Keep in mind the structure that you set up for your team and the leader you place in charge will have complete control over the outcome. For maximum effectiveness, it should be clear by now that a multidisciplinary leader possesses a distinctive vantage point that uniquely equips them to coordinate collaborative teams. Their diverse background positions them as adept conductors, creating symphonies in the orchestra of collaborative endeavors.

Case Study: Google

Google is widely recognized for its multidisciplinary approach to problem-solving. The company's teams are made up of experts from different fields, such as engineering, design, and marketing. This diversity of knowledge and expertise allows the company to approach problems from multiple angles and come up with new and innovative solutions. Google's co-founder, Larry Page, is known for his multidisciplinary background in computer science and business, which helped him lead the company to success, allowing him to understand the technical aspects of the business *and* understand its commercial and strategic aspects. He is also known for his ability to think strategically and make decisions that align with the overall goals of the company, helping him build an enterprise that is now one of the most valuable in the world.

When we think of Google, the eponymous search engine immediately comes to mind. However, the operation behind that search engine has significantly impacted numerous aspects of our lives that we may not even be aware of. Google's multidisciplinary approach has been instrumental in solving complex problems across various sectors, including healthcare, retail, manufacturing, finance, and transportation.

In healthcare, Google has contributed to improved patient outcomes and cost reductions. By using machine-learning algorithms to analyze vast amounts of medical data, doctors can now identify patterns and predict patient outcomes more efficiently. Google's expertise in computer vision has led to the development of a diagnostic tool capable of detecting diabetic retinopathy, a leading cause of blindness in diabetic patients.

In the retail sector, Google's machine-learning algorithms have been employed to optimize pricing and inventory management, enabling retailers to better understand consumer demand and improve supply-chain efficiency. Furthermore, Google's expertise in mapping and location services has resulted in tools that help retailers better understand consumer behavior and enhance their store layouts.

Google's influence extends to manufacturing as well, where their methods have led to increased productivity and improved operations. Machine-learning algorithms optimize production schedules and enhance quality control, enabling manufacturers to reduce costs and increase efficiency. Additionally, Google's expertise in computer vision has facilitated the development of inspection systems that can automatically identify and correct defects in products.

The finance sector has also reaped the benefits of Google's multidisciplinary approach, harnessing algorithms that analyze vast amounts of financial data, allowing banks to identify patterns and predict customer behavior. Google's expertise in natural-language processing has led to the creation of chatbots that assist customers with their banking needs, further streamlining the process.

Lastly, transportation companies have seen improvements in operations and efficiency thanks to Google's methods, optimizing logistics and routing, helping reduce costs and increase delivery speeds. Google's expertise in mapping and location services has also provided tools that allow transportation companies to better understand traffic patterns and plan more efficient routes.

Creating Collaborative Teams

Collaborative teams are an increasingly fundamental part of modern organizations. These teams, consisting of people with diverse skills and expertise, collaborate harmoniously to tackle problems, share knowledge, and develop innovative solutions. As with any great undertaking, building an effective collaborative team requires a clear purpose, well-defined goals, and meaningful metrics to measure success.

Before assembling a collaborative team, it's essential to establish a clear purpose and set specific goals that the team can work towards. This helps team members focus their efforts on a common aim, while also ensuring that the team's work aligns with the organization's overall strategy and vision.

Once a purpose has been established, it's time to put together a diverse team with a range of skills and expertise. A successful collaborative team is like a mosaic of individuals, each with their unique backgrounds, skills, and expertise. When choosing team members, consider their functional expertise, problem-solving skills, and ability to collaborate. Embrace diversity in gender, race, age, and experience to create an inclusive and innovative team culture.

Next, it's crucial to establish clear roles and responsibilities within the team. Every team member should know their role and how their skills contribute to the team's overall success.

This clarity helps prevent confusion and ensures that everyone is working towards the same objectives. It also promotes accountability, as team members can be held responsible for their actions.

To keep track of the team's progress, set metrics based on specific objectives, including quantitative measures like revenue growth, cost savings, project completion rates; or qualitative measures such as customer satisfaction or employee engagement. Regularly reviewing and discussing these metrics with the team will help maintain focus and drive continuous improvement.

A strong foundation for any collaborative team is open communication and collaboration. Encourage team members to share ideas, knowledge, and expertise, creating an environment where everyone feels comfortable contributing. This can be achieved through regular team meetings, brainstorming sessions, and the use of collaborative tools and platforms that facilitate information sharing.

Of course, to ensure the success of a collaborative team, ongoing support and resources are vital, including access to necessary tools, technology, and training, as well as backing from senior management. Demonstrating management's commitment to the team helps build trust and motivation among team members, encouraging them to take ownership of their work and contribute to the team's overall success.

Encourage Communication and the Open Exchange of Ideas

Open communication plays a crucial role in fostering teamwork and cross-functional thinking. By cultivating an environment where employees feel comfortable sharing their thoughts, ideas, and concerns, organizations can increase the likelihood of effective collaboration. One way to do this is by establishing clear channels of communication, such as regular meetings, group messaging platforms, and email distribution lists, to keep employees informed and connected. Furthermore, creating a safe space for feedback can encourage employees to share their thoughts and opinions without fear of judgment or negative consequences. Training employees to listen attentively and respectfully to their colleagues also helps foster a supportive atmosphere where everyone feels heard and valued.

Another key aspect of cross-functional thinking and problem-solving is the exchange of ideas and knowledge. Organizations can facilitate this exchange by encouraging brainstorming sessions where employees can present ideas and discuss potential solutions to challenges. Developing mentorship programs, where experienced employees are paired with newer hires, can also facilitate knowledge transfer and skill development. Moreover, providing opportunities for professional development, such as training, workshops, and seminars, can expand employees' skillsets and encourage growth.

Lastly, celebrate the team's achievements and encourage learning from setbacks. Recognizing and celebrating accomplishments, both big and small, is essential for maintaining motivation and promoting a positive team culture. Equally important is learning from setbacks and using them as opportunities for growth and advancement. By fostering a culture of continuous learning and improvement, collaborative teams can become more resilient, adaptive, and innovative, ready to face any challenge that comes their way.

Incorporating teamwork and collaboration into employee performance metrics ensures that these skills are considered and rewarded during performance evaluations. Finally, promoting employees who demonstrate exceptional teamwork and cross-functional thinking reinforces the importance of these qualities for organizational success.

By embracing open communication, encouraging the sharing of ideas and knowledge, and rewarding collaboration and teamwork, organizations can foster a culture of cross-functional thinking that will help them thrive in an ever-changing business landscape.

Establishing Shared Goals

In the quest for organizational growth and innovation, it's crucial to recognize the potential pitfalls that silos, or vertical arenas of specialization, can create. Throughout this book, we've emphasized the importance of stepping outside your lane in order to truly make an impact. Staying within the confines of your department, even if you're disruptive, may not lead to significant progress. Instead, it's important to challenge these divisions and dare to cross the barriers between departments, as this can enhance collaboration, communication, and overall productivity.

To dismantle these silos, everyone in the organization needs to work towards the same objectives. This can be achieved by establishing shared goals, involving employees from different departments in the goal-setting process, and ensuring clear communication of these goals to everyone. Start by defining your organization's purpose and the long-term outcomes you hope to achieve. This vision should be simple, inspiring, and easy to communicate.

In order to promote a sense of ownership and involvement among employees, invite those from various departments to participate in the goal-setting process. Organizing workshops, brainstorming sessions, or focus groups can help gather input and ideas from different teams, fostering cross-departmental understanding and creating goals that are relevant and achievable. With a clear vision in place, break it down into specific, measurable, achievable, relevant, and time-bound (SMART) goals to ensure that everyone understands the objectives, the means of measuring success, and the time frame for achieving these goals.

Transparent and effective communication is critical for the success of any organization. Once you've established your shared goals, make sure they're communicated clearly throughout the organization through various channels, such as company-wide meetings, intranet updates, and email newsletters. Regular updates help keep employees engaged and motivated to work towards the shared vision.

However, breaking down silos involves more than just establishing shared goals. It also requires creating a culture that encourages collaboration and open communication between departments. To do this, implement initiatives that promote cross-departmental interactions, such as team-building activities, cross-functional projects, and opportunities for informal networking. Encourage managers to model collaborative behavior and create an environment where employees feel comfortable sharing ideas and seeking input from colleagues in other departments.

To further encourage collaboration, recognize and reward employees who actively engage in cross-departmental efforts. Acknowledging their contributions not only motivates them to continue working collaboratively but also inspires others to follow suit.

Training

Before implementing any training and development programs, it's crucial to identify the essential skills needed for success. Communication, collaboration, problem-solving, adaptability, and conflict resolution are often among the most important skills for employees to master. Clear and concise information sharing, working together towards common goals, identifying issues and implementing the best course of action, openness to change, and addressing disagreements are all vital components of a successful team and ones that every member needs to master.

Once you've identified the essential skills for cross-functional success, develop a comprehensive training program that addresses these skills and tailor it to the unique needs of your organization. Offer self-paced e-learning courses that cover essential cross-functional skills and that can be accessed from anywhere. Organize in-person or virtual workshops that focus on specific cross-functional skills, such as effective communication or collaboration techniques, providing an opportunity for employees to practice skills in real-time.

Pair employees with experienced coaches or mentors who can provide personalized guidance and support, and help them refine and apply their cross-functional skills. Incorporate team-building activities and exercises to encourage collaboration and strengthen interpersonal relationships among employees.

Training and development should not be a one-time event. Encourage employees to continue learning even after they've completed the initial training programs. Offer constructive feedback on performance in collaborative teams, helping employees identify areas for improvement, and track their progress over time. Create a culture of learning by encouraging a mindset of continuous education and development. Share success stories, provide resources for further learning, and recognize employees who demonstrate improvement in cross-functional skills. As employees grow in their abilities, provide more advanced courses and workshops to help them continue honing their skills.

By fostering a culture of continuous learning and development, organizations can equip their employees with the skills needed to excel in collaborative teams. This will improve individual performance and contribute to the overall success and growth of the organization.

Communication

Technology has provided us with a multitude of tools to help break down barriers, enabling a more cohesive and effective work environment. One such tool is instant messaging platforms like Slack, Microsoft Teams, or Google Chat. By offering real-time communication, these platforms can bridge the gap between departments and foster efficient information sharing. To fully harness their potential, organizations should encourage their employees to utilize these platforms for work-related discussions and questions. Creating dedicated channels for specific projects or teams can also help keep conversations organized and streamline collaboration. Integrating instant messaging with file-sharing services further enhances communication and promotes knowledge sharing across the organization.

In addition to instant messaging, video conferencing platforms like Zoom, Microsoft Teams, or Google Meet can help bring employees together, regardless of where they are located. By fostering a sense of connection and teamwork, these platforms can play a pivotal role in breaking down information silos. Organizations can also use video conferencing for brainstorming sessions, problem-solving, and project updates to keep everyone informed and engaged. Encouraging the use of video helps establish personal connections and build trust among employees, further promoting a collaborative work environment.

Collaboration software, such as Trello, Asana, and Basecamp can also help organizations tackle the issue of silos by providing a streamlined platform for managing projects and tasks. These tools offer visibility into ongoing work, helping prevent redundancies or miscommunications. Integrating collaboration tools with other platforms can create a cohesive digital workspace, promoting even greater efficiency. To make the most of these platforms, though, organizations should assign clear roles and responsibilities, ensuring everyone knows their tasks and deadlines. Encouraging regular updates and feedback within the platform can help maintain accountability and open communication among team members.

Finally, establishing a centralized knowledge repository, like an internal wiki or shared document library, makes it easier for employees to access the information they need. Organizing content by department, topic, or project facilitates quick and easy access to relevant data. Encouraging employees to contribute their knowledge and expertise fosters a culture of collaboration and knowledge sharing. Regularly updating and maintaining the repository ensures it remains relevant and accurate, benefiting the entire organization.

Celebrating Success and Recognizing Contributions Across Departments

The success of any company lies in the hands of its employees. It's through their collaboration and teamwork that great things are achieved. Recognition and celebration play a crucial role in fostering a sense of shared achievement and creating a positive culture. When employees feel valued, they're more likely to work together toward common goals. Furthermore, such recognition increases employees' sense of self-worth and satisfaction, leading to higher morale and productivity. A positive work culture where employees feel appreciated is also more likely to retain top talent and reduce turnover. Finally, when employees feel supported and recognized for their efforts, they're more likely to take risks and think creatively, leading to new ideas and innovations.

When it comes to celebrating successes, there are several practical approaches to consider. One is creating opportunities for public recognition, such as company-wide announcements, newsletters, or award ceremonies, ensuring that the efforts of employees from different departments are acknowledged and appreciated throughout the organization. Establishing a regular recognition program, such as an "Employee of the Month" award or an annual recognition event, ensures that celebrations become an integral part of company culture. Encouraging peer-to-peer recognition is another great way to foster camaraderie and shared accomplishment. Implementing a peer recognition program or creating a platform for employees to give shout-outs to their colleagues, can facilitate this.

Incorporating celebrations into company events can create fun and memorable experiences for employees while reinforcing the importance of teamwork and collaboration. By doing so, you'll help build a sense of shared accomplishment and create an environment where employees feel valued, motivated, and inspired to work together toward common goals.

Multidisciplinary Harmony and Balance

In leadership, having varied experiences is like owning the ultimate toolkit. A multidisciplinary leader is like a maestro leading a band. They can guide both multidisciplinary and interdisciplinary teams, much like a skilled conductor who brings together different musicians to create beautiful music.

Imagine the multidisciplinary team as a band where each musician has their unique style, and the leader is like the conductor who encourages everyone to play their best while collaborating with the rest of the band.

Now, think of interdisciplinary teams as different music genres coming together to create a fusion track. In this scenario, the multidisciplinary leader is like a music producer who ensures that all the musical elements blend seamlessly into a catchy tune.

But the game-changer? The magic of cross-disciplinary thinking—the ability to mix different musical genres, just like a DJ creating a remix. By combining various styles strategically, they encourage interactions that lead to more exciting and powerful results. Just as various instruments interact to enhance the overall sound, cross-disciplinary thinking enables a leader to strategically blend different knowledge domains, fostering interactions that lead to more profound and powerful accomplishments.

By embracing this creative approach, a multidisciplinary leader can create an environment where diverse ideas come together, innovative solutions flourish, and the company finds its groove towards a more successful future. The leader's role isn't just about directing; it's about composing a hit that maximizes the team's potential, taking the organization to new heights.

JOURNEY MILEPOSTS

- **Purpose and Goals:** Defining a clear purpose and goals is essential for building an effective collaborative team. Have you ever been part of a team without a clear purpose? How did it affect the team's effectiveness?

- **Team Diversity:** A successful collaborative team is diverse, consisting of individuals with different backgrounds, skills, and expertise. Reflect on a diverse team you've been a part of. How did the varied backgrounds and skills enhance or challenge the team's success?

- **Roles and Responsibilities:** Clear roles and responsibilities help prevent confusion and promote accountability. Can you recall a situation where unclear roles led to confusion or conflict? How might it have been handled differently?

- **Metrics and Objectives:** Setting metrics based on specific objectives helps maintain focus and drive continuous improvement. How have specific metrics guided your past project? Were there ever times the metrics seemed misaligned with the true objectives?

- **Communication and Collaboration:** Think about a time when poor communication affected a project's outcome. How might open communication have changed the result?

- **Learning Culture:** How has celebrating achievements (or reflecting on setbacks) influenced your personal growth or the growth of teams you've been a part of?

- **Performance Metrics:** Open communication and collaboration are crucial for fostering teamwork and cross-functional thinking. How would incorporating teamwork into your performance metrics influence your work behavior?

- **Shared Goals:** Establishing shared goals that are simple, inspiring, and easy to communicate can help align everyone in the organization towards the same objectives. Can you think of an inspiring shared goal that truly aligned a team you were part of? Why was it effective?

- **Cross-departmental Involvement:** Involving employees from different departments in the goal-setting process can foster cross-departmental understanding and create relevant and achievable goals. Have you experienced the benefits of involving various departments in goal setting? What insights or challenges did this bring?

- **Effective Communication:** Can you pinpoint a moment when transparent communication transformed a potentially negative situation into a positive one?

- **Departmental Achievements:** Celebrating achievements and learning from setbacks helps create a culture of continuous learning and improvement. Reflect on a time when your department's achievement was celebrated. How did it influence the team's morale and motivation?

17

Breaking Down Silos: Fostering Cross-Disciplinary Thinking

The reason why it is so difficult for existing firms to capitalize on disruptive innovations is that their processes and their business model that make them good at the existing business actually make them bad at competing for the disruption.
— Clayton Christensen[1]

Success requires an organization to operate as a cohesive unit, not a series of separate cost centers or silos, but as a single unified entity. This requires breaking down silos and building a culture of cross-functional thinking.

A silo mentality refers to a situation where employees work only within their respective departments, leading to a lack of communication, collaboration, and knowledge sharing across

---

[1] Christensen, C. M. (1997). The Innovator's Dilemma: When New Technologies Cause Great Firms to Fail. Boston, MA: Harvard Business School Press.

different parts of the organization which, in turn, leads to inefficiencies, duplication of effort, and a lack of innovation.

Companies need to tear down the silos. Employees who collaborate with colleagues from different areas of expertise can learn, sell, and develop skills more quickly. Innovation is increasingly reliant on interdisciplinary cooperation, rapid digitalization, and cross-border collaboration, demanding executives who can effectively lead projects at these intersections. The importance of horizontal teamwork cannot be overstated.

IKEA and Apple have proven the immense value of cross-functional and multidisciplinary approaches. These companies have boosted profits, improved product development, increased employee engagement and retention, reduced time to market, and enhanced customer satisfaction by breaking down silos and promoting effective teamwork. But while these approaches have immense potential, they require developing cross-disciplinary skills and promoting cross-disciplinary thinking to unlock their full potential. By doing so, individuals and organizations can create a more dynamic and innovative environment, enabling them to solve complex problems more effectively.

Cool Companies, Cooler Collaboration

IKEA and Apple exemplify these benefits. Making IKEA products involves a process that includes designing products, finding materials, shipping them, making the products, distributing them, selling them, and getting feedback from customers.

Apple's unique and easy-to-use products and interfaces also involve understanding what customers want, creating the product, manufacturing it, promoting it, and delivering it. In both cases, teams work together instead of one after the other. They think and work together instead of working on separate parts and passing them along.

Research shows that cross-functional teams can boost profits by 23-25%, but sadly, 75% of such teams are dysfunctional due to confusion of purpose, miscommunication, and a failure to reconcile individual silos and cost centers within a business.[2] Leaders of such teams often lack expertise in the multiple disciplines involved, and often fail to appreciate the burdens of all of the disciplines in the room which can result in unproductive meetings.

According to a study by Harvard Business Review (HBR) in 2016,[3] cross-functional teams can improve product development speed and quality by 20-30%. That's a significant improvement! By bringing together people from different functional areas, cross-functional teams can identify and address issues that might not have been apparent to someone with a narrower perspective.

But that's not all. Cross-functional collaboration can also increase employee engagement and retention by 50%, as stated

---

[2] Wuchty, S., Jones, B. F., & Uzzi, B. (2007). The increasing dominance of teams in production of knowledge. Science, 316(5827), 1036-1039.
[3] Harvard Business Review (HBR). (2016). Why Cross-Functional Teams Are More Than Twice as Likely to Exceed Financial Targets. https://hbr.org/2016/06/why-cross-functional-teams-are-more-than-twice-as-likely-to-exceed-financial-targets.

by Deloitte in 2017.[4] When employees feel like they're part of a team that values their contributions and encourages collaboration, they're more likely to be happy at work and stick around for the long haul.

According to the same HBR study, another benefit of cross-functional teams is the reduction of time to market by 25-50%. This is because cross-functional teams have a more streamlined decision-making process and can quickly identify and resolve issues.

In addition to these benefits, cross-functional teams can enhance customer satisfaction and loyalty by 20-30%, as stated by HBR in 2016. By bringing together people with different backgrounds and expertise, cross-functional teams can create solutions that are more effective and better suited to the needs of customers.

But cross-functional teams aren't the only way to improve productivity and innovation. Multidisciplinary teams can also bring a lot to the table. According to a study conducted by Wuchty et al. in 2007,[5] multidisciplinary teams can lead to more patents, higher citation rates, and greater impact in scientific research. This is because such teams have a broader range of knowledge and skills, which allows them to approach problems from different angles and come up with more innovative solutions.

---

[4] Deloitte. (2017). The Rise of Cross-Functional Teams.
https://www2.deloitte.com/content/dam/Deloitte/us/Documents/human-capital/us-cons-hc-the-rise-of-cross-functional-teams.pdf
[5] Wuchty, S., Jones, B. F., & Uzzi, B. (2007). The increasing dominance of teams in production of knowledge. Science, 316(5827), 1036-1039.

IKEA and Apple have achieved great success creating teams outside of the standard chain of command. These teams, led by top executives with unique job titles like Chief Digital, Risk, or Innovation Officer have members with specialized skills who work together to complete projects. They report to leaders who may not have the same backgrounds but share a common goal of achieving the assigned capability and completing all projects related to it. Rather than just managing projects, the traditional departments focus on providing specialized guidance and learning opportunities for the staff assigned to these capabilities.

Multidisciplinary teams can also bring benefits by approaching problems from different angles and fostering creativity and innovation. Multidisciplinary research can increase the probability of breakthrough innovations by up to 64%,[6] while cross-disciplinary teams can address complex societal challenges that require expertise from multiple fields.[7]

Make the Coolness Your Own

How can you leverage these approaches in your own work? The key is to develop cross-functional, cross-disciplinary, and multidisciplinary skills. By learning about different areas and fields of knowledge, you can bring a more well-rounded perspective to your work, leading to better problem-solving,

---

[6] Lakhani, K. R., Lifshitz-Assaf, H., & Tushman, M. L. (2013). Open innovation and organizational boundaries: task decomposition, knowledge distribution and the locus of innovation. HBS Working Paper, 13-080.
[7] National Academy of Sciences. (2005). Facilitating Interdisciplinary Research. https://www.nap.edu/catalog/11153/facilitating-interdisciplinary-research

more innovative ideas, and a greater ability to work effectively in teams.

IKEA and Apple have showcased the immense potential of cross-functional and multidisciplinary approaches in achieving organizational success. By improving communication, collaboration, and innovation, they have developed groundbreaking products while reducing errors, redundancies, and delays. Developing skills in these areas and working effectively in teams can make employees invaluable assets to any organization.

A key factor in unlocking the full potential of these approaches lies in promoting cross-disciplinary thinking over mere multidisciplinary collaboration. This involves breaking down silos and fostering a culture where managers, leaders, and team members integrate ideas from various disciplines, rather than remaining confined to their areas of expertise. The key to success lies not just in one's knowledge but in effectively combining it with the knowledge of others.

While both multidisciplinary and cross-disciplinary individuals possess skills and knowledge from multiple fields, the critical difference lies in the integration of these fields. Cross-disciplinary thinkers actively synthesize ideas from diverse disciplines, generating new insights and solutions, whereas multidisciplinary individuals keep their areas of knowledge separate. Cross-disciplinary thinking fosters a more dynamic and innovative environment, enabling organizations to solve complex problems more effectively.

In my experience, cross-disciplinary thinkers make more effective generalists than their multidisciplinary counterparts. By embracing cross-disciplinary thinking, individuals can create a more fluid, dynamic environment where innovative ideas emerge and thrive. When people allow their lanes to be flexible, they enable the potential for groundbreaking solutions and discoveries. Emphasizing cross-disciplinary thinking over multidisciplinary collaboration can help organizations unlock their full potential, solve complex problems, and innovate more effectively.

Clayton Christensen's concept of disruptive innovation has become a cornerstone in the world of business, transforming the way companies and industries approach growth and competition. A renowned Harvard Business School professor and author, Christensen argued that successful companies often fail to remain competitive because they fail to recognize and adapt to disruptive innovations.

Disruptive innovation, as defined by Christensen, is a process in which a product or service starts at the bottom of the market and then moves up, eventually displacing established market leaders. Unlike sustaining innovation, which focuses on improving existing products, disruptive innovation creates new market opportunities and reshapes industries. It often occurs when new entrants in the market, armed with lower-cost business models, capture underserved and overlooked segments of the market. As these new players continue to improve their products or services, they eventually start to compete with, and even surpass, the established market players.

Creating and implementing disruptive innovation requires a diverse team of individuals who can collectively think outside the box and challenge conventional wisdom. There are several reasons why teamwork plays a critical role in fostering disruptive innovation:

- **Diversity of perspectives:** A diverse team brings different viewpoints, experiences, and expertise to the table, enabling the team to approach problems from various angles and to identify unique solutions that may not have been considered before.

- **Encouragement of risk-taking:** A supportive team environment fosters a culture that embraces risk-taking and experimentation. Team members feel more comfortable sharing unconventional ideas and taking calculated risks, knowing they have the support of their colleagues.

- **Synergy:** Teams that work well together can achieve more than the sum of their individual efforts. The collaboration of team members allows them to tackle complex problems more effectively, resulting in more innovative solutions.

- **Communication and adaptation:** A successful team communicates openly and adapts to changing circumstances. In the face of disruptive innovation, this ability to adapt and evolve is crucial for a company to stay competitive.

By fostering a diverse, supportive, and communicative team environment, companies can better position themselves to identify, develop, and implement disruptive innovations that can reshape their industries and pave the way for sustainable growth.

Take a moment to consider the power of this opportunity in your everyday operations. Having a multidisciplinary leader in these roles allows for someone with a more fluent understanding of the multiple silos to organize, communicate, and conduct the activities between the disciplines, allowing for seamless cross-functioning. Does your team already have multidisciplinary leaders just waiting for the opportunity to show you what they can do?

When people from different areas of expertise work together in a team, it can lead to many benefits for organizations. IKEA and Apple are great examples of companies that have achieved tremendous success by using cross-functional and multidisciplinary approaches. By working together, they improved communication, collaborated better, and brought innovative products to the market, while also reducing errors, redundancies, and delays. Many organizations are increasingly embracing cross-disciplinary teams as a way to foster innovation and address complex challenges in their own organizations.

JOURNEY MILEPOSTS

- **Breaking Down Silos for Cohesion:** How can your organization challenge the existing 'silo mentality'? Think of ways to promote cross-departmental communication, collaboration, and knowledge-sharing to foster a more cohesive and innovative work environment.

- **Value of Cross-Functional Collaboration:** Diversity of perspectives, encouragement of risk-taking, synergy, communication, and adaptation are critical factors for a successful cross-functional team. Considering the significant benefits, such as increased profits, improved product development speed, and enhanced customer satisfaction, how can your organization better incorporate cross-functional teams? What barriers might be holding you back, and how can they be overcome?

- **Multidisciplinary vs. Cross-Disciplinary Thinking:** While both multidisciplinary and cross-disciplinary approaches bring value, the latter involves a deeper integration of diverse knowledge. How can your organization move from merely multidisciplinary collaboration to true cross-disciplinary thinking?

How might this shift open doors to more groundbreaking solutions and innovations?

- **The Power of Disruptive Innovation:** Clayton Christensen's concept points to the significance of recognizing and adapting to disruptive innovations to stay competitive. Reflect on the role your team plays in fostering or inhibiting disruptive innovation. How can you encourage a culture of diversity, risk-taking, synergy, and adaptation to pave the way for sustainable growth?

- **The Potential of Multidisciplinary Leaders:** Do you recognize potential multidisciplinary leaders within your organization? Consider the value of having leaders with a comprehensive understanding of various silos to foster seamless cross-functioning. How can you create opportunities for these individuals to showcase their abilities and contribute to the organization's success?

18

Champions of Integration: Multidisciplinary Leaders

When a person has access to both the intuitive, creative and visual right brain, and the analytical, logical, verbal left brain, then the whole brain is working ... And this tool is best suited to the reality of what life is, because life is not just logical—it is also emotional.
— Stephen Covey

Peter Senge, a renowned organizational theorist and author, introduced the concept of the learning organization in his seminal 1990 work, *The Fifth Discipline: The Art and Practice of the Learning Organization*.[1] Senge's theory emphasizes the importance of continuous learning and adaptation for organizations to thrive in a rapidly changing world. A key aspect of his philosophy is the role of leadership in fostering a learning environment, particularly when it comes to leading collaborative teams.

---

[1] Senge, P. M. (2020). The Fifth Discipline: The Art & Practice of the Learning Organization. Revised Edition. Currency.

Peter Senge's Fifth Discipline offers valuable insights for leading multidisciplinary teams effectively. By embracing systems thinking and fostering a learning environment that promotes open dialogue, shared vision, and continuous improvement, leaders can maximize the potential of their teams and drive their organizations towards success.

The Fifth Discipline

The Fifth Discipline, or systems thinking, is the cornerstone of Senge's learning organization theory. It refers to the ability to see the interconnections and patterns within a system, rather than focusing solely on individual parts. By understanding how different components of an organization interact and affect each other, leaders can better manage complexity and facilitate effective decision-making.

Systems thinking is particularly relevant when leading multidisciplinary teams, as it enables leaders to appreciate the diverse perspectives and skills that team members bring to the table.

When leading multidisciplinary teams, Senge's Fifth Discipline offers valuable insights that can help leaders foster collaboration, innovation, and continuous learning:

- **Cultivate a shared vision:** Senge emphasizes the importance of creating a shared vision among team members. A clear, compelling vision that is collectively understood and embraced by all team members encourages alignment and commitment, driving the team towards a common goal.

- **Encourage open dialogue:** Facilitating open dialogue among team members allows for the exchange of diverse perspectives and ideas, fostering creativity and innovation as well as identifying and addressing potential issues and conflicts.

- **Embrace diversity:** Recognizing and valuing the unique skills and expertise of each team member is crucial in multidisciplinary teams. By leveraging the diversity of the team, leaders can facilitate more effective problem-solving and decision-making, ultimately leading to better outcomes.

- **Foster a learning environment:** A critical aspect of Senge's learning organization philosophy is the emphasis on continuous learning and improvement. Leaders must create an environment where team members feel comfortable sharing their knowledge, learning from each other, and experimenting with new ideas, enabling the development of innovative solutions and strategies.

- **Promote systems thinking:** Encouraging team members to think in terms of systems rather than in isolated components can help them identify patterns and relationships that may not be immediately apparent. This holistic perspective enhances collaboration, improves problem-solving capabilities, and enables the team to better adapt to changing circumstances.

To successfully lead such teams, leaders must adopt a more flexible, adaptable, and collaborative approach that values the unique perspectives of team members from various disciplines. To address these challenges, leaders should work with other leaders and stakeholders to break down organizational barriers and promote cross-functional collaboration, advocate for the team's needs and goals at higher levels of management to secure necessary resources and support, and encourage a culture of experimentation and learning, where team members are empowered to take calculated risks and learn from failures.

Who Should Lead a Collaborative Team?

As I discussed above, the leaders of these teams need to be outside of the silo structure. Putting someone who is entrenched in a silo at the head of a collaborative team will create an undesirable emphasis on the silo from which they came.

Simply placing someone from your C-suite or second-level management in charge of a multidisciplinary or cross-disciplinary team isn't going to work either. The person in charge of the collaborative team will only encourage cross-disciplinary thinking when that individual is one who understands the nature of the beast. The person in charge must be able to communicate with each discipline on their own terms, understand the constraints and issues that each discipline presents, and balance the role of upper management against the production of the team. Sometimes, as is the case with Apple and IKEA, you need to put someone in charge who is separate and distinct from the C-suite.

It's through these leadership roles that the organization can best leverage the unique skills of multidisciplinary individuals. As we have discussed throughout this book, the collaborative team leader brings a wealth of diverse knowledge, skills, and perspectives to the table, which can be harnessed for the team's success. But perhaps most importantly, the multidisciplinarian is a quick study. By nature, they have used both sides of their brain, and they will process and synthesize information with the team better than would someone from a specialized silo or department.

Multidisciplinary leaders are able to see the bigger picture and understand how different functions and teams can work together to achieve common goals. These leaders play a crucial role in:

- **Bridging communication gaps:** Multidisciplinary leaders can effectively communicate with different teams, ensuring that each department understands the objectives and expectations of the organization as a whole. They can also facilitate the sharing of knowledge and ideas between departments, promoting a culture of collaboration.

- **Encouraging collaboration:** By promoting cross-functional thinking, multidisciplinary leaders can help break down silos that may have previously existed within an organization. This fosters an environment where employees from various departments work together, combining their unique skills and expertise to solve problems and create innovative solutions.

- **Driving innovation and growth:** When employees from different departments collaborate and share ideas, the resulting synergy can lead to the development of innovative products and services that drive organizational growth. Multidisciplinary leaders play a pivotal role in ensuring that this collaborative environment thrives, thus enabling the organization to remain competitive in the market.

When done effectively, innovation and growth will flow from the ideas and efforts of the team. The leader acts as a conductor, encouraging each member to put forth their best effort.

The Otherworldly Power of Collaborative Teams

NASA's space exploration missions are a prime example of the power of collaborative teams. By bringing together experts from different fields, such as engineering, physics, and medicine, NASA is able to approach problems from multiple angles and generate new and innovative solutions. The diversity of knowledge and expertise within these teams is what allows NASA to push the boundaries of space exploration.

Charles Bolden, former Administrator of NASA, is a testament to the benefits of having a multidisciplinary background as a leader. As a retired astronaut and Marine Corps general, Bolden possesses a unique understanding of both the military and space exploration industries. His military background provided him with the leadership and management skills required to lead such a large multidisciplinary organization, while his background in space exploration gave him a deep understanding of the technical and scientific aspects of the mission.

As a multidisciplinarian, Bolton was able to draw experiences from all of his lanes to better lead the teams that he worked with. He was not stuck in a lane or focused on a single direction. He was a cross-disciplinary juggler capable of great things.

Bolden is also known for his ability to balance competing priorities and communicate effectively with both technical and non-technical stakeholders. This was instrumental in leading NASA through some of its most successful missions, including the Mars rovers and the International Space Station. It's a clear demonstration that a leader with a multidisciplinary background can excel in leading complex and ambitious projects.

NASA's multidisciplinary approach has proven to be highly effective in solving complex problems and achieving success across a wide range of industries. Some real-world examples include:

Aerospace industry: NASA's multidisciplinary approach has helped the aerospace industry solve complex problems related to aerodynamics, propulsion, and materials science. For instance, NASA's aerodynamics expertise has helped develop new technologies that have improved the efficiency of air transportation and reduced fuel consumption.

Healthcare: NASA's expertise in developing new technologies has resulted in the development of medical equipment and devices. Collaboration with medical professionals has led to the development of new training programs and medical procedures for extreme environments, such as space or remote locations. NASA's expertise in materials science and biotechnology has also helped advance the field of regenerative medicine.

Energy: NASA's expertise in energy management and efficiency has been applied to various industries, leading to the development of more efficient and sustainable energy systems. For example, NASA has worked with companies to develop new technologies that can capture and store energy from renewable sources, such as solar and wind power.

Environmental science: NASA's multidisciplinary approach has helped advance our understanding of the Earth's climate and the impact of human activities on the environment. NASA's expertise in remote sensing, atmospheric science, and earth science has helped develop new technologies for monitoring and mitigating the effects of climate change.

These are just a few examples of how NASA's multidisciplinary approach—and Bolden's multidisciplinary leadership—has helped companies and organizations in various industries solve complex problems and achieve success. Through its partnerships with industry, NASA continues to make a significant impact on the world and drive progress in numerous fields.

Fostering Multidisciplinary Leaders

Developing and encouraging multidisciplinary leaders is crucial for organizations looking to break down silos, promote cross-functional thinking, and achieve lasting success. By providing employees with the training, support, and opportunities needed to develop their skills across different departments, organizations can foster a culture of collaboration and innovation that drives growth and competitiveness.

Leading a cross-disciplinary team can be challenging, but it also offers a wealth of opportunities for innovation and growth. By adopting a flexible leadership approach, addressing corporate constraints, leveraging the unique skills of multidisciplinary individuals, and cultivating trust and empathy, leaders can help their teams overcome challenges and unlock their full potential for success.

Organizations can foster the development of multidisciplinary leaders through several strategies.

- **Cross-functional training:** Provide employees with opportunities to work in different departments and gain exposure to various functions within the organization. This can be done through job rotations, cross-functional project teams, or temporary assignments to different departments.

- **Training and development programs:** Offer comprehensive training and development programs that cover a wide range of topics, including leadership, communication, problem-solving, and strategic thinking. These programs should be designed to equip employees with the skills needed to excel in cross-functional roles and contribute to the overall success of the organization.

- **Mentoring and coaching:** Pair employees with experienced mentors or coaches who can provide guidance and support as they develop their multidisciplinary skills. This can help employees gain valuable insights and perspectives from seasoned professionals who have experience working across different departments.

- **Recognize and reward:** Celebrate and reward leaders and employees who demonstrate exceptional cross-functional skills and leadership abilities through performance reviews, promotions, or other incentives that recognize the value of multidisciplinary thinking and collaboration.

By fostering leaders with experience and skills across different departments, organizations can facilitate better communication, collaboration, and overall success. Multidisciplinary leaders play a crucial role in bridging communication gaps by effectively communicating with different teams, ensuring that each department understands the objectives and expectations of the organization as a whole. They can also facilitate the sharing of knowledge and ideas between departments, promoting a culture of collaboration with an effective level of balance.

To tap into this potential, the leadership team of the organization should recognize and appreciate the unique value of each team member and encourage them to share their expertise and insights. They should foster an environment of continuous learning and development, where team members are encouraged to broaden their skill sets, explore new disciplines, and implement collaborative problem-solving techniques, such as design thinking or the Agile methodology, which allows team members to contribute their diverse skills and perspectives to address complex challenges.

Last, but certainly not least, the organization should cultivate trust and empathy. Building trust and empathy within a cross-disciplinary team is crucial for fostering collaboration and ensuring the team's success. Invest time in getting to know each team member's background, strengths, and perspectives. Encourage team members to share their personal stories and experiences, which can help build empathy and understanding. Finally, promote transparency in decision-making and communication, so that team members feel heard and included in the process.

By embracing the Fifth Discipline of systems thinking, leaders can better manage complexity within multidisciplinary teams and maximize their potential. Multidisciplinary leaders, with their ability to see the bigger picture and process information holistically, play a pivotal role in bridging communication gaps, encouraging collaboration, and driving innovation and growth.

Beyond Linear Boundaries

The multidisciplinary leader will recognize when something from one domain should be thrust into another to make an innovative leap. When a skilled multidisciplinary leader conducts her team as an orchestra conductor arranging music and picking and choosing which instrument to use, her cross-disciplinary thinking will propel innovation and forward motion toward success.

In the 1960s, Maltese psychologist Edward de Bono coined the phrase lateral thinking. De Bono developed this concept as a form of creative problem-solving that encourages one to look at situations from fresh new angles and unconventional perspectives. At this moment, having read most of this book, I hope that statement alone conjures images of multidisciplinary people taking a holistic approach in problem-solving, strategic planning, and innovation.

De Bono considered the key to lateral thinking as thinking outside the box. He saw it as a way of finding shortcuts, alternative routes, or even redefining the problem in its entirety. The theory behind lateral thinking made it clear that his goal was to encourage thinking or acting in ways that might seem illogical or absurd as a means of sparking new ideas.

Lateral thinking encourages the use of random words or stimuli to find connections that people might not think are immediately obvious. De Bono encouraged the holistic approach and using counterintuitive viewpoints as well as challenging established beliefs and considering that the accepted way might not be the only way, nor may it be the best way.

Because of their diverse backgrounds, multidisciplinary leaders are much more adept at seeing everything from the lateral perspective. Their broad range of experience in multiple fields allows the multidisciplinary person to be more comfortable in the face of ambiguity. As a lifelong learner, and a master of integrating conflicting and contradicting ideas and methods, a multidisciplinary leader ignites and fuels the fire of lateral thinking.

When someone has experience in multiple lanes, they are more prone to draw lines between seemingly unrelated concepts. Such people do not fear randomness, and they are more willing to take the risk of doing something uniquely different. The Jack of all trades is a master of lateral thinking and a master of integration. It is their nature.

The Swiss Army Knife Leader

Multidisciplinary leaders are the ultimate integration champions! They have a natural ability to unite people from all sorts of backgrounds and making it work harmoniously. When it comes to breaking down barriers between different departments or fields, multidisciplinarians talk the talk and walk the walk. These leaders are the glue that holds everything together.

They are magical at getting people to share their ideas, blend their strengths, and come up with innovative solutions that nobody could've thought of on their own. They have an uncanny ability to see the big picture to connect the dots between different parts of a project or issue.

Multidisciplinary leaders are like the Swiss army knife of leadership—adaptable, innovative, and ready to take on whatever comes their way. They are the integration wizards who can make magic happen!

JOURNEY MILEPOSTS

- **Shared Vision:** Senge emphasizes the importance of a collectively embraced vision. Reflect on a time when you were part of a team with a clear shared vision. How did that influence the team's dynamics and outcomes? Conversely, consider a situation where the vision was not clear. What challenges did that present?

- **Value of Diversity:** Recognizing the unique skills and perspectives of each team member is central to multidisciplinary success. Can you think of an instance where a diverse set of skills and perspectives led to innovative solutions? Or perhaps a time when a lack of diversity impeded progress?

- **Role of Leadership:** The leadership needs of collaborative teams differ from traditional ones. From the book's insights, evaluate how siloed leadership structures can inhibit the power of cross-disciplinary teams. Do you agree with the idea that leaders of such teams need to be outside the conventional structures?

- **Case Study: NASA:** Reflecting on NASA's success with collaborative teams, consider how organizations you are familiar with could replicate this approach.

What key elements from NASA's strategy could be applied to other industries or projects?

- **Cultivating Multidisciplinary Leaders:** Consider the strategies provided for fostering these unique leaders. Which of these strategies do you believe would be most impactful in your organization or industry? Why?

- **Trust and Empathy:** Think about the teams you have been a part of. How has trust, or a lack thereof, influenced the team's function and outcomes? How can organizations institutionalize the cultivation of trust and empathy in their team-building strategies?

19

Embracing All Lanes: Your Symphony of Discovery

Jazz, like leadership, combines the unpredictability of the future with the gifts of individuals.
— Max De Pree

As we draw the curtains on this journey through the world of multidisciplinarity, I invite you to reflect on the transformative power of thinking in multiple lanes. From the depths of our mindset to the heights of innovation; along the paths of who we are, what we do, and how we think; we have travelled a landscape that champions versatility, adaptability, and the boundless potential of the human mind.

I have shared not just concepts, but fragments of my soul—little anecdotes, experiences that shaped my perspective. I hope they resonated with you, not just as stories, but as living testaments to the power of a multidisciplinary mindset.

Allow yourself to give in to your curiosity and explore new lanes of travel and new domains. Allow yourself to become a lifelong learner who looks at the world in a holistic and embracing manner. You want to see everything, so stop and look. Take time to smell the roses because you may learn something. Becoming a multidisciplinarian creates a mindset that is always ready to grow and to learn. It is this fertile mind that will motivate you to want to learn more and be more.

The more you learn the more you will realize that your abilities are not set in stone. What you do and who you are can be cultivated through diligence and dedication.

You will see challenges differently. Problems will become exciting moments where everything you know floods to the mind and all your disciplines kick into gear so you can find the perfect solution. You will embrace challenges. You'll see setbacks as steppingstones to success. And you will face the unknown with an eager desire to learn what's ahead. You will persist when the path is daunting.

Being a multidisciplinarian is just the beginning.

Your Swiss Army Knife of Tools

Being a generalist gives you a leg up on so many different levels. As you go forward, I want you to truly grasp the essence of our shared journey—a journey celebrating the myriad paths of knowledge and disciplines. Embracing being a generalist is clearly the path of a lifelong learner. It's also the path of someone who can find excitement in anything.

By embracing being a generalist, you're not just indulging an intellectual whim.

You have permission to live your life.
You will be a one-person collaborative team.
You can innovate when others replicate.
You will thrive when others only survive.
You will see challenges as opportunities.
You will see uncertainty as adventure.
You have set yourself free.
You will never conform to rigid boxes.
You don't just adapt; you pioneer.
You no longer just think; you explore the reaches of your mind.
You will never be done experiencing life.
You will never be bored again.
You will see the unknown as a learning opportunity.
You can forge connections of ideas, thoughts, and disciplines.
You will not fear a new domain.
You can dance between the boundaries of knowledge.
You can—on moment's notice—ignite the flames of creativity, critical thinking, and problem-solving.
And I hope you feel empowered to do something that I didn't list. If you do, please reach out to me and let me know.

Setting Sail on Your Journey

As you reflect on what you have read—or, more importantly, what you have thought as you read—remember that cross-disciplinary thinking isn't just a too, it's a superpower.

Cross-disciplinary thinking allows you to see connections that other people miss. It gives you the ability to juggle domains and introduce a little bit of this and a little bit of that into every action you take.

I hope you're prepared to begin your new journey as you immerse yourself in generalist philosophy. Dive into a new hobby, strike up a conversation with someone whose life melody is different from yours, or maybe, just maybe, pick up a book on a subject you never imagined you'd explore.

And remember, you're not alone. Share your insights, your experiences, your challenges. There's an entire community out there eager to listen, learn, and grow alongside you.

A Musical Interlude: Your Symphony

Now that we're almost done, please indulge me in a visual metaphor. Pause for a moment. Reflect upon the whole of your life's experiences, expertise, and passions. Think of your spectrum of knowledge as an orchestra, a collection of disciplines creating beautiful music together, like a symphony.

Now imagine a conductor. The orchestra is your life, everything you ever were, everything you are now, and everything you will ever become. The conductor stands upon your curiosity and the undying quest for knowledge that propels you through the myriad lanes of multidisciplinarity. Stand on that podium and look at your entire life to see how all of your disciplines work together in harmony.

The conductor is the "why" that fuels your journey. Why do you do what you do? What drives you? What motivates you? The conductor is that inner calling that drives you to orchestrate a symphony of life experiences, knowledge, and the unyielding spirit of exploration.

The conductor's baton orchestrates more than just melodies. It evokes the harmonious interplay of diverse disciplines, each having its distinct note, yet blended as one creating a sound that resonates with who you are. With each sweep of the baton, your purpose and ambitions pull the notes from each of your areas of expertise, careers, and hobbies to make amazing music. Your symphony is a reflection of the harmonic integration of your experiences, thoughts, and the never-ending dance between the known and the unknown.

Take a moment now and then to tune the instruments, to revisit and reflect on the evolving sheet music of your professional life. The tunes may change, new instruments may join, and some may take a bow, but the music plays on, resonating with the richness of your multidisciplinary journey.

Every time you jump into a new discipline or take on a new role, remember: You're not just adding a note, but composing a melody in the grand symphony of your professional existence.

As your "why" changes, and your purpose becomes more defined, you will fine-tune your conducting skills and improve your ability to find the magic as you merge the notes of your life seamlessly together. And then, one day, you will introduce a note from a random discipline and create something that is so powerful it might just change the world.

(To help you better visualize your orchestra, you can download a short workbook and symphony diagram from my website at www.JoeCurcillo.com/symphony.)

Celebrate Your Multitudes

Remember what Walt Whitman said: *Do I contradict myself? Very well then I contradict myself, (I am large, I contain multitudes.)*

Embrace the multitudes within yourself, for they are the keys to unlocking a more fulfilling and rewarding life. I encourage you to adopt the practice of looking back on your day and asking yourself, *What did I learn new today?* When you spend your whole day knowing this question is coming, you will find something to learn to avoid disappointment when you rest your head on the pillow.

Thank you for joining me on this journey. As we come to a close, I want you to consider everything that we've discussed, and all of the benefits of being a multidisciplinary generalist.

Before we part, close your eyes for a moment and tell yourself: *I am an ever-evolving tapestry of knowledge. In diversity, I find strength. Every discipline, every field of study, every interaction is a new lens through which I view the world.*

May your path be illuminated by the crossroads of disciplines, and may your mind forever dance in the zone of limitless possibilities. You are now living the *Generalist's Advantage*. Embrace it. Cherish it. And most of all, let the symphony of disciplines light your path.

JOURNEY MILEPOSTS:
Your Swiss Army Knife

Consider the "Swiss army knife" of skills, knowledge, and approaches that you bring to the table. Here are a few probing questions to guide your reflection:

- **Diversity of Tools:** What distinct disciplines or fields have influenced your leadership style, and how do you seamlessly integrate them into your decision-making processes?

- **Sharpen Your Blades:** In which areas do you feel you need further refinement or learning to enhance your multidisciplinary leadership prowess?

- **The Missing Blade:** Are there any disciplines or perspectives that you might be overlooking or undervaluing, and how might they bolster your leadership capabilities?

- **Integration vs. Isolation:** How do you ensure that your multidisciplinary approaches complement one another, rather than clash or compete?

- **Evolution of Your Toolkit:** As the landscape of leadership continually evolves, how do you keep your "Swiss army knife" updated, ensuring that you're equipped with the most relevant tools for the challenges of tomorrow?

Acknowledgements

I celebrate myself, and sing myself,
And what I assume you shall assume,
For every atom belonging to me as good belongs to you.
— Walt Whitman

First and foremost, I thank my family. Living with my diverse interests, business plans, and crazy ideas is like being on a roller coaster without safety belts.

Next is Lindsay Adam, OAM. My brother from Down Under. The six years plus of consistent Wednesday afternoon chats and debriefs have made me a better person and kept me on track with all I do.

I am grateful for the unwavering support and commitment of my executive assistant, Nicole Holley. She is always there for me.

I thank my editor, Jason Liller, for tolerating the many incarnations of this book that I threw at him. He worked through many chapters that did not see print.

I will be forever grateful to Moshe Botwinick, PhD. A true inspiration in my journey into mentalism as well as my deep dive into the minds of generalists.

I would like to thank several good friends who have always offered in-depth guidance and support. You were sounding boards for my ideas and thoughts through the process of writing and defining this book. Thank you to my executive suite team of John Wetzel, Jason Reimer, Mike Perry, James Mapes, and Jeff Haste. The five of you possess leadership skills that are second to none. Working with each of you has made me a better leader and thinker..

Finally, I thank my friend, mentor, and fellow magician Mark Levy for giving me a swift kick in the butt. He encouraged me to embrace my multidisciplinary nature and my expertise in cross-disciplinary thinking. Without him, this exploration would never have launched.

About the Author

Meet Joe Curcillo, the visionary author behind *The Generalist's Advantage*. As the CEO of Generalist's Advantage Strategies, Joe is the Maestro of Integration, weaving together the diverse threads of his multidisciplinary expertise to craft innovative strategies that transcend the boundaries of personal and business silos.

With a career that reads like a symphony of success, Joe has mastered the art of thinking across disciplines. From his former life as a trial attorney to his roles as a CEO, civil engineer, strategic advisor, government operative, author, fine artist, psychic entertainer, and magician, Joe's journey is a testament to the power of cross-disciplinary thinking.

In *The Generalist's Advantage,* Joe shares the secrets of his integrative approach, empowering you and your team to tackle complex challenges with finesse. His guidance will equip you with the tools you need to infuse cross-disciplinary thinking into every facet of your organization, propelling you to new heights of innovation and success.

Joe doesn't just talk the talk; he walks the walk. With his wealth of real-world knowledge and a track record of excellence in diverse fields, he'll show you how to adapt and thrive in today's dynamic business landscape. By focusing on sustainable growth and agility, Joe Curcillo prepares you for a future where you're always a step ahead of the competition.